Six Stages
of a
Pastor's Life

Creative Leadership Series

Six Stages of a Pastor's Life

J. Keith Cook & Lee C. Moorehead

Creative Leadership Series
Lyle E. Schaller, Editor

Abingdon Press / Nashville

SIX STAGES OF A PASTOR'S LIFE

This book is printed on acid-free paper.

Library of Congress Cataloging-in-Publication Data

Cook, J. Keith, 1935–
      Six stages of a pastor's life/J. Keith Cook & Lee C. Moorehead.
        p. cm.

      ISBN 0-687-38558-X (alk. paper)

      1. Clergy—Office. 2. Pastoral theology. I. Moorehead, Lee C. II. Title.
BV660.2.C66   1990
253'.2—dc20   89-28389
                                          CIP

Lines from "Stopping by Woods on a Snowy Evening" on p. 100 are from *The Poetry of Robert Frost*, ed. Edward Connery Lathem, copyright © 1970 by Holt, Rinehart, and Winston, Inc. Used by permission of The Estate of Robert Frost; Henry Holt and Co., Inc.; and Jonathan Cape Limited.

A portion of chapter 6 was suggested by Lee C. Moorehead's article "Recycling the Retired Minister," which originally appeared in the January 1987 issue of *The Christian Ministry*.

MANUFACTURED IN THE UNITED STATES OF AMERICA

To my wife, Ruth Ollis Cook

—J. KEITH COOK

For my wife, Betty,
and our children—
David Bruce, Deborah Lee,
Rebecca Ann, Timothy Lucas

—LEE C. MOOREHEAD

Foreword

For most of us, the calendar is a supplemental tool for recalling something that happened a few years ago. Instead of dating that memory by the year in which it occurred, we usually do it by where we were or what we were doing at that time. Where was I in school when that happened? Was it before I married? Were we living in that small apartment or in a house? Before or after Becky was born? While Laura was still at home? Or after she had left for Oklahoma? After we have made that association, we begin to fix the year.

In a parallel phenomenon, pastors outline their memories by which congregation they were serving when a certain event occurred. As the years roll past at an increasingly rapid pace, life begins to resemble a series of chapters in a book. The first chapter is life at home before going away to school. A second, and for many one of the most enjoyable and memorable, is the emancipation that came with going away to school. The third may be that first pastorate—and for many, that was in Gopher Gulch.

Eventually comes that last chapter. For some it is a lengthy one labeled *retirement*. For a few, it is a brief one called death—at an unexpectedly early age. For a growing number, such as the co-author of this book, Lee Moorehead, what had appeared to be one final chapter already is so filled with exciting challenges that it must be divided into at least three separate chapters—one labeled "Community Church," a second titled "Batavia." A third, which does not yet have an outline, much less a title, may be called simply "Retirement, Finally."

The thesis of this book is that many of us reflect on our lives by dividing them into chapters or stages. In like manner, the professional career of the minister can be divided into chapters or stages. This book represents an effort by two experienced and remarkably effective parish pastors to reflect on six stages of a ministerial career.

That arbitrary number was dreamed up by three people sitting in an office in Nashville, Tennessee, many months ago. *Six* was chosen, not because it is a perfect number, but because it is fairly easy to identify six distinctive stages in a ministerial career. Perhaps the easiest to define is that first call or appointment. For many, that is where an approach to "doing ministry" in a parish setting is formed. The second easiest to identify, for those who choose it, is the part-time ministerial workload accepted by many pastors in the first years of retirement.

Between those two stages are several others. For the truly itinerant preacher, this may mean reliving the same chapter twenty times in twenty different locations. For most pastors, however, each stage is different from the one before and the one that follows. Perhaps the most subjective of these is the one titled "The Best Years."

Ideally, every pastor would apply that title to the current stage, but for many, one pastorate or one stage stands out as *best*. For a few, the best years are always ahead, out beyond reach, and never arrive. For those more fortunate, every pastorate is the best, and it is impossible to describe one as *very* best.

This book is intended for five audiences. The obvious one is today's pastor, who will nod affirmatively while reading the chapters that describe the earlier stages in ministry and study more carefully the chapter that reflects contemporary reality.

In a second audience is the person about to embark on a career in the parish ministry, who seeks an annotated road map which offers informed and wise advice on what to do, how to do it, and pitfalls to avoid in the years ahead.

A third audience includes pastors who are nearing the end of the trail, who will enjoy this wise and structured means of reflecting on their experiences, will interrupt their reminiscing with an enlightened "Aha!" as the light dawns, and will be challenged by the last two chapters on what can lie ahead.

The fourth consists of those lay people who are married to pastors—those who seek a better understanding of what their spouses are experiencing now and are curious about what the future may bring.

A fifth audience includes dedicated lay leaders who recognize that no other vocation resembles the pastoral ministry, who seek a better understanding of what their minister has experienced in the past and also may be curious about the stages that lie ahead. Many of these committed people are members of a congregation usually served by a minister in stage one or two or five, and this book may help them or their Pastoral Relations Committee to be a more effective support group for their minister. This could be useful recommended reading for every new member of that committee.

Plato advised us that the unexamined life is not worth living. This book will help readers examine and reflect on each stage of a pastorate.

Lyle E. Schaller
Yokefellow Institute
Richmond, Indiana

Contents

Introduction

In *Necessary Losses*, Judith Viorst describes many of the things each of us must give up. The first is the womb, so comfortable and protective. Departure is jarring. But the loss is necessary if we are to live and grow.

The move from school to parish can be like that. By the time we have made it through college and seminary, or their counterparts, we know how to "do" school. We've grown accustomed to the friends, the community, and the resources available for work and leisure. So the first field out of school may be a tough one to plow. The move away from this womb can be jolting.

So many decisions must be made the first time around—decisions that affect our lives and the lives of those around us. Some of us have more options, some of us have fewer, depending upon many factors: the nature of the placement system of our denominations, the current need for pastors, and—let's face it—our own personal "marketability." Some graduates are more sought after than others. We're not talking about what should be, but what is. In most denominations the need for pastors is greatest in small churches in small communities. In some systems, we are placed; in others, we seek and are sought. There are many variables.

And the difficult decisions are by no means over once we

land somewhere the first time. Even the rare minister with a career-long first parish must make decisions about that. Every move and every stage in this vocation present a struggle toward decision, and that includes preparation for and entry into retirement.

We are Lee C. Moorehead and J. Keith Cook. Lee is a retired but active minister in The United Methodist Church. He has served as associate pastor and pastor in Ohio, Illinois, and Wisconsin, and as a faculty member at St. Paul School of Theology in Kansas City. Lee continues to lead preaching workshops and to serve in other ways.

Keith has served as pastor of three Presbyterian (USA) churches in Nebraska in his thirty years of ministry; he also directs a school for one hundred or more pastors each summer, leads seminars, and is a consultant.

Both of us have published books on preaching and the practice of ministry. In this book, Lee has written chapters 4, 5, and 6. Keith has written this introduction and chapters 1, 2, and 3. We identify ourselves in this way to allow for the clearly personal styles and references made in this co-authored work.

We will address several stages of a pastor's career life. It is impossible to cover the various stages and opportunities of every minister's career. But perhaps the relatively common ones discussed here will help clergy to ask their own questions and look for other help with their own big-stage changes and the inevitable minichanges for course correction.

Clearly, the first and often most treacherous stage is the period immediately following seminary or Bible college. There are so many ways to go. Do I want to be a so-called solo pastor? Can I do it out there all alone? Or should I be an associate pastor? Maybe I'm cut out to be a campus pastor, or a pastor in some other form of specialized ministry. What if I attempt to handle two kinds of work at the same time—be a part-time pastor and a part-time something else? What are some of the considerations in making those and other choices? Our hope is that the reader will find some help here.

One of a pastor's problems is the struggle to keep a good balance between two enormous pressures—career and the needs of one's personal life, which includes a family for some of us. All ministers have had to struggle with this problem—or should have. The reader either has reached that stage of life, or will, and here we offer some beginning guidance for that important stage.

Another major moment for many of us is the time when we feel directed toward—or just wonder about—taking a different fork in the road. Someone asks us to consider leaving the parish to work in the "head office," to be an executive type. Maybe we would like to specialize in counseling, or perhaps we feel we should aim for the senior pastor position in a large congregation. Should I specialize or be a generalist? There are many things to think about in regard to such options, and we will get into those.

For some of us, the next significant stages are those that usher us into our second, third, or fourth parishes, into mid-career. What does that hold for us, in terms of both problems and opportunities? These will be discussed in chapter 3.

Many of us finally begin to feel that we have reached a stage in our career when everything seems easier. Some would define that time as the best years, and one might wonder why one should read anything about it. Why fiddle with a good thing? But even blessings need thoughtful stewardship—there was a problem tree in Eden. There are dangerous temptations during the best of times, and here we take a look at some of the opportunities and challenges that might arise.

At age twenty-five, during the first month of Keith's first parish, he began to develop strategies for retirement. It is never too soon to study that stage, and we include a chapter on planning for retirement.

Finally, we offer some suggestions for the decisions one

must make during retirement. Can I live where I have loved the people and been loved, or must I move out of town? It's a tough question. Can the church still use me in some way that makes use of years of good experience? There are several issues.

We cannot ask all the questions, nor can we supply all the answers to even the questions we propose. Our hope is that we can offer some insight from our own experiences and observations. We would be pleased if these chapters do what they were intended to do: stimulate your continued search for whatever seems best for you. God calls us to do what we do best, but we sometimes need to think and pray in order to find the honest indications of that call.

I

The Post-seminary Period

The movers back up to your school apartment one June day. And what a difference that day makes! You are entering a whole new world—a new world with several stages. Those stages will vary in substance and length, but one stage is certain—that first job right out of school.

In that first stage, many of us find ourselves solo pastors of small churches. Others become assistants or associates in larger situations; or, alone or in teams, in arrangements that include two or more congregations; or in some form of specialized ministry. Each situation has its own issues.

Pastoring Alone

Traditionally, a young male graduate would go to his first church as its pastor. He probably was the only person on the staff—preacher, teacher, counselor, secretary, mimeograph operator, and maybe custodian.

He "should" have had a wife, and the couple needed to give every evidence of being perfectly married. The wife was seen as her husband's helper. She would play the piano, teach a Sunday school class, and might serve as the unpaid, unofficial, director of Christian education. She was expected to be active in the women's organization and might soon be its president. She also cleaned the church office, because it probably was in their residence. And this is still true for almost half of us.

Some things, however, have changed. More of those pastors are women now. Sadly, this is true in part because churches find that they can pay a female in the pulpit less—inappropriate as that may be. Congregations are like individuals, in that economics, more than almost anything else, has the power to quickly adjust theology, prejudice, and politics.

But members of churches that have their "druthers" still often look for a male pastor with a wife and a "nice" family. Often acting on the images of their formative years, they want the residents of their parsonages to model life's structures as they wish them to be.

However, as congregations are "cornered" into having women as pastors, they are discovering—much to their surprise—that women often are better preachers than men. So many women have been through major life experiences, such as divorce, that they are better able to connect with the feelings of hurting parishioners. They are more willing to talk about their feelings. They know how to pastor.

Solo pastors are more frequently single than in the past. Many congregations have discovered that great gifts for ministry can be brought to parish work by singles. But still most churches seek married pastors, especially for solo and senior pastor situations. It is easier for people to see singles in the role of associate or assistant pastor. Increasingly, the solo slot is divided so that a couple can fill the one position. Some solos can be sung as duets.

There also has been a sharp increase in the number of second-career clergy. Congregations often have more confidence in such people, anticipating that they have broader applicable experience and more maturity. Parishioners tend to believe that ministers are ignorant and impractical in other than biblical, theological, and ecclesiastical matters—that they don't know the "real" world. Studies conducted by Drew University indicate that because of this notion, seminary graduates who are second-career persons often are more easily accepted and therefore make a more effective transition to parish ministry.* Others can do it and do it well, but second-career people have a leading edge.

Anyone who goes solo does need to face the preferences of churches, and also needs to plan on spending up to four years in making appropriate adjustments to local expectations. There are always exceptions, but in the main, the preference, though less fierce than formerly, continues to be for a married male. And racial and cultural similarity tend to be preferred. For example, Nebraska congregations doubt that a native New Yorker can be adequately transplanted, although it can happen; a south-to-north movement is easier than a north-to-south.

Prejudice against lack of experience also often exists. Many of the smallest churches in the least attractive locations expect experienced pastors. They forget that few graduates get their first call as senior pastor of Riverside Church in New York, hoping to someday pastor at Crossroads Church in Gopher Gulch, Oklahoma. Gopher Gulch deserves good pastoring, but it may need to be a proving ground rather than the goal.

Let's go to Gopher Gulch for a moment. Any newly ordained minister may land there, and it can be both devastating and wonderful. It can be lonely. It may be that the only person in your age range is your spouse, and if you are not married—or not happily married—what then? It may be that conversations center on crops and the price of hogs—the real stuff of rural life—and all you know is Tillich and theater. It feels far away from the camaraderie of classroom days.

Add to that the awkward truth that excellence in the classroom, which you may have achieved, requires a different set of competencies from those of the parish. And increasingly, seminary graduates who have grown up in

*Janet F. Fishburn and Neill Hamilton, "Seminary Education Tested by Praxis," *The Christian Century* (February 1-8, 1984), pp. 108-12.

19

larger churches in cities must now pastor in small churches in villages. The people there know more about you than you know about them, because they watch television and they read. It can be a terrible time for those who cannot or will not adjust.

It can be a bad time, too, for those who cannot cope with the way members of smaller congregations see their churches. Their loyalty is to the church, not to the pastor, unlike what you may have grown up with at big old Marble Grove Church, where the senior pastor was powerful and honored. These good people in Gopher Gulch see pastors come and go. Some they love, and some they don't—depending almost entirely upon whether the pastor genuinely loves them. They will give some power and authority to any pastor whose love they can truly trust; *none* to those whose affection they cannot count on.

The church in Golpher Gulch will survive you. Its members will wait you out if they must, but they will retain control. For one thing, they have among themselves people who have nowhere else to exercise power. They realize that if they can't maintain control, the rapid succession of ministers, with their varying ways, will keep their church off-balance. Small rural churches often appear dead, but they seldom roll over and die. They are tough. A few denominations take action to close them, but without that force, internal local powers will help a church hold on for a long time. A pastor who threatens that control, or who doesn't seem to understand it, will not count for much. The one who works lovingly with it will discover that the pastor does have authority.

A practice-of-ministry professor may have told you that a well-structured church has a bevy of committees. Gopher Gulch never heard of and doesn't care about those committees. That's not how the people here do things. Their board works as a committee of the whole for every issue. They don't want their system fiddled with—partly because they understand their time-tested system, and partly because they fear they may not understand a new one. Also, what they have is *their* system, and to change to an outsider's system suggests a transfer of power to the "owner" of the new system. They don't like that. It doesn't sound as if it will work, and so, of course, it won't.

Or it may be that a denominational bureaucrat is urging the new minister to make a change at Gopher Gulch, and the parishioners there resist. They dislike being managed by a newcomer minister, and they like even less being managed by some outside executive. If necessary, they will just wait until you leave, and then they will go back to the way that works for them.

A pastor who knows these kinds of things and remains lovingly patient with those people can be blessed at Gopher Gulch. In fact, it can be a tremendous place to be. The folks there are just folks. They hope and they hurt. They laugh and they love. They are people, like any other people. Separated from the warm seminary womb during that first stage, the pastor mature enough to not feel superior will live and grow at Gopher Gulch.

The people will be most forgiving of your early "grade C" sermons. They will help you discover which kind of preaching helps people, and which doesn't. The church used to be the main source of counseling, especially in smaller communities. Mental-health services have reached rural areas now, but even so, some people feel they cannot afford psychotherapists. Or they still may be too far from a counseling clinic. So they talk to you. As a result, in your first four years as a pastor in Gopher Gulch, you learn counseling skills that will stay with you for the full forty.

Not every small church is in a rural area, of course. Some exist in the city and have the advantage of access to a wider variety of resources. It is easier in the city to be a private person during personal time and during private troubles. It is surprising, however, how often one is recognized in stores or the library, even in Megapolis. In the aisles of Walmart on one's day off, one will hear about the illness of a parishioner's aunt. And there can be loneliness, too, even in the city.

The sense of competition with colleague congregations and their pastors can be very discouraging if your church seems to succeed. On the other hand, disregard of you is noticeable if your church does not seem to be going anywhere. Your small church may be in a changing neighborhood, and if you can't effect a pattern of growth, or at least stability, you can easily feel like a failure. It's worse if your parish is not growing, even though it is in a booming suburb or a "renewing" section of the city!

Or you may be called to solo a new suburban church from scratch. Then you'll *really* learn the meaning of the word *solo*. A district or conference may have voted to start the new church and patted you on the back with such sounds of symphony that you felt the whole orchestra backing you. But now here you are, going door to door, putting a parish together by yourself. That's a *real* solo—a cappella, yet!

In all these situations, a good student of ministry will learn numerous skills for a lifelong calling. People everywhere need to hear the comfort and the challenge of the Word of God.

Associate and Assistant Positions

When you are an associate or assistant to a senior pastor, it is a little like being married. If you "marry" the right one, there is nothing quite like it—and if it's the wrong one, there still is nothing quite like it!

A staff position in a larger church has much to offer. You are likely to be located in a larger community, with the advantages many of us have come to enjoy. Better equipment and more support staff, such as secretaries, probably are available. It is a "comfort zone" for those of us who grew up in urban congregations. We know how to function in that territory. Never is the full weight of the congregation's success on your shoulders. The buck stops in the office of the senior pastor.

If your task was well thought out, you will be doing mainly what you do best and little of what you do less well. Whereas your classmate who is now a solo pastor somewhere will be learning by doing it all, you will be learning by doing some of it and watching an old hand do the rest of it. Either way has value. To do our work, we probably learn about one-fourth of what we need to know in school, two-fourths in our first four years in the ministry, and the final fourth during the remainder of our vocational life. So our decision to be good students in those first four years is critical.

One may "marry" the right or the wrong senior pastor, but either way, that pastor has much to teach about ministry. One minister tells of spending his first years with a lousy senior pastor, but he decided to be a loyal friend. They walked, lunched, and chatted together for four years. He learned many good things to do and things not to do in ministry. He made the best of an otherwise bad situation. The wise associate or assistant will decide to be a loyal friend, if at all possible.

Now, it does happen that some associate or assistant pastors find that they do little more than run errands. If you find yourself in such a situation, you need to have a talk with the senior pastor, difficult as that may be. Be as up-front and nonthreatening as possible, putting the emphasis not on how bad the senior is, but on how you need that senior to give you more responsibility so that you can learn to carry out a life of ministry.

Senior pastors are among the loneliest of pastors. Loyalty and friendship are mutual needs. Rugged individualism is a fine thing, unless you're on a rowing team, in which case it can be disastrous—for everyone. Lock-step agreement is not the only option, nor would that be useful. There must be room for honest variation in viewpoint and style. I would never, for example, want to put down my wife in public, nor she me, because we're a team. I willingly advocate my wife's interests and needs when appropriate—even though I may not fully agree with her—because we have a commitment to each other. And she frequently is my advocate. Pastors on a staff need to be willing to work in that way. Unless they do, both congregation and pastors suffer, and the gospel witness is weakened. A congregation responds in kind to the quality of relationship it perceives among its pastors.

If I could give six words of advice to my fellow senior pastors, they would be these: advocate, advocate, advocate, and include, include, include! Advocate before the congregation's officers each year for generous salaries and other provisions for the other pastors. Advocate for them when they seem to have stepped into too deep water. Don't let them drown out there all alone. Include the other pastors in planning, thinking, goal-setting, and information.

And if I could offer six words of advice to associate and assistant pastors, they would be these: work, work, work, and report, report, report! The senior pastor will not be credible or successful when advocating support of an associate who seems lazy, is always late, or appears ineffective. Associates/assistants who do not keep their seniors well informed about what they are doing and what is happening to members of their parish is inviting division. A minister who is unwilling or unable to deliver in these ways should look for some other position.

In being considered as an associate or assistant, you might address the following essential questions:

1. Is your title to be Associate or Assistant? What is the perceived distinction and the implications? If the title is Assistant, does it become Associate by some specific date? Typically, an associate is viewed as having a more secure status. In some denominations, an assistant can be fired by simple action of the senior pastor and/or the church officers, whereas some procedures protect the associate from such precipitous decisions.

2. How long does the senior pastor plan to stay? What

happens to you, should that pastor leave? Often the rest of the staff is expected to leave soon after the senior departs.

3. In the company of the search committee or church officers, if possible, have the senior state the specifics of his or her role as advocate for you at annual salary-review time.

4. Ask for a written list of expectations, including a note that states where the power to adjust that list in the future lies—with the senior pastor, the personnel committee, or the church board. Such a list cannot cover all bases, but it must be a minimal definition of what you must be sure to do and what you must be sure not to do.

5. To whom do you report? Who is your supervisor? Who will review your work? Ordinarily, it would be the senior pastor, working closely with a personnel committee.

6. How many hours per week are you expected to be on the job, and what free time is planned? One would expect to work at least forty-eight hours per week, have a full day off each week, and two to four weeks' vacation each year. Forty-eight on-duty hours is a fair minimum expectation, although many pastors and other professional persons work more than fifty-five.

Multiple Arrangements

One kind of pairing is marital. Sometimes one congregation is served by a clergy couple, or one pastoral position in one church may be served jointly, on a shared-time basis, by a couple. In such cases, life can become quite complicated, yet each can work. Often such arrangements provide the only way congregations can be adequately pastored or clergy couples can fulfill their call and still stay together.

Another common pairing is congregational, and a variety of these kinds of link-ups exist. In the most usual, two or more congregations in one community or more are served by one pastor or by a team of pastors. These churches usually are denominationally related.

Some denominations have what they call federated

churches—two or more churches of differing denominations in one community, which worship and work as one, though each maintains its affiliation with its parent denomination. Such multidenominational congregations rarely experience numerical growth, and denominational leaders usually discourage their formation.

Pastoring more than one congregation provides some of the same predicaments you might face if you were married to several spouses at the same time. As a pastor of two or more churches, you had best be prepared to work deliberately to make each congregation feel as loved as the other(s). If you are married, which congregation will your spouse join? Will there be jealousies in the "nonchosen" congregation(s)? If you have an office in one town, will the parishioners in the other town(s) come to see you? Is there any rivalry between the congregations or between their communities?

How do you arrange special services, such as a Christmas Eve midnight Communion service? There is only one midnight per day. What if a perfectly balanced salary package is undone next year, when one church feels it can offer a raise and the other cannot? Instead of one board of officers, there are two or more. The youth groups won't want to merge, so double the time load. Add the miles between the towns. It gets to be time consuming and complicated—but it can be done. I spent my first decade serving a two-point field in small rural towns. And I felt loved—mostly. That is where I learned how to be a pastor.

If the congregations are of different denominations, add a whole new layer of meetings. There is a need to understand and relate to the denominational system of each communion, and that need must be met with integrity, if all the parishioners are to feel you are their pastor.

Specialized Ministry

Counselor. Chaplain. Educator. Campus minister. Writer. Church consultant. Denominational executive. And there are others. God calls some of us to other than parish work, but most of the options for specialized forms of ministry are not open until we have had the front-line experience of one or more pastorates. There is one major exception: women ministers in some denominations frequently go directly from seminary into work such as counseling or campus ministry. Some women graduates make early entry into denominational administrative or program work. Others find themselves in recruitment work for colleges or seminaries, or as staff for church-related caucus groups.

There are cautions and handicaps in this type of ministry. For one thing, recent reports suggest a decrease in specialized opportunities, except for the growth in evangelical parachurch organizations. Also, some people will say that you "couldn't hack it" in the parish, so you had to go another way. But none of us can do all forms of ministry well. Parish work may be the most common form, but it should never be thought of as the *only* honorable form. Still, that attitude does affect some clergy in specialized ministry; there can be a feeling of bitterness.

Ministers in specialized work often need to be intentional about their congregational, denominational, and faith connections. Some ordained counselors, consultants, and others never go to worship; don't tithe; expect the support of their church but do not support it; want the endorsement of their denomination but do not engage in the work of their conferences, districts, or presbyteries. There can be anger about that, and ministers in specialized work who later want to go into parish work often find it difficult to find acceptance.

But there are blessings. Weekends and evenings may be free, there is less cajoling of "little old ladies"—and more important, it presents an opportunity to minister in line with a special ability you may have. All these issues need to be weighed, and no one can resolve them for another individual.

The Bivocational Career

At one time, many pastors held down two jobs. This was called tent ministry, patterned after the Apostle Paul, who supported his evangelizing by making and selling tents. My father was a home builder, and his crews often included a minister, who raised his family on the earnings of his carpentry work. But he felt his calling to preach the Word. The church provided him with a home and a modest "love offering" from time to time, and when area farmers butchered, he'd receive some frozen meat.

The practice was common. It provided a ministry for many small churches that could not afford to support full-time pastoral services, and it gave many men a chance to follow their call, especially in the numerous small independent fundamentalist churches that dotted the land.

Now there has been a return of this practice. Today in America, sixty thousand or more bivocational ministers in many denominations are following their call. It is a real option for congregations of modest means, and good ministers may want to serve where they feel needed. But they require other financial support, so they use an old skill or seize a new opportunity to add to their income. For example, one might pastor part-time and write computer programs for businesses in the community.

Before considering this type of arrangement, be sure the congregation is fully apprised and agreeable. Everything must be aboveboard. One "full-time" minister who felt underpaid held a full-time second job as a mail carrier for over a year without the congregation's knowledge. His city was so large that this could easily happen. When church members phoned, his wife would say he was visiting the hospital.

The congregation wasn't paying him well, but they did think they had a full-time minister. That had been the agreement. His actions were clearly dishonest, and the resulting anger and disillusionment were too damaging on many fronts. It is critical that all parties agree to such an arrangement.

Make sure that any other line of work you may enter is compatible with the Christian ministry. Moral and ethical standards, as well as conflicts regarding obligations and the use of time also must be considered. I know a minister who is also a mortician. Both the church and his mortuary business are small. He and the congregation have agreed that when the church has a funeral, it will be put first, whether it is related to his mortuary or another, while his mortuary is entrusted momentarily to his employees. He remains available for counseling when called upon. This minister keeps entirely faithful to that agreement, and it works.

If a minister is called to ministry, it is important that it not become a sideline. It will take some teaching of the congregation and some integrity on the part of the pastor, but it can be done. The bivocational pastor needs to attend all the congregational events it is possible to attend in order to touch base with parishioners. It is critical that the members feel that their minister wants to be with them and loves them, even though a second job takes some of their pastor's time.

We have reviewed the main categories of service available to each of us in our first stage of ministry. Decisions made at this time affect the rest of our lives and ministries. But there are other life-directing issues which also are part of the two-fourths of learning that takes place in this first stage of ministry.

First, learn how to "care for the quo" (as in "status quo"). It can't be said too often that people hate change. I have known many discouraged pastors who say, "Am I the first pastor who ever wanted to do more than 'cuddle the quo' in this parish?" While a congregation courts you, it may express a desire for creative change. What these people usually mean is that they want the youth to like the church more—as it is—and that they want to grow in size, without current leaders needing to move over, and without in-place policies and practices being questioned by newcomers. They seem to want a minister who will bless the present state of affairs, rather than one who will challenge, create, and move the congregation toward a new vision. Sermons may be most appreciated if they confirm what the parishioners already know, and you may be needed only to marry and bury, help the Sunday school, and organize a vacation Bible school. The message is often, "Don't change anything."

That is normal. The pastor's challenge is to learn how to lead the flock past those barriers. Declaring war on the congregation is not the way to do it. Things will change. Nothing can stay the same. But it is essential that the only changes made are those that are important, needed, and effected with care. People are rarely angered into loving more. They can only be *loved* into loving more. Every pastor has to somehow learn the art of being an intentional agent of planned change from within the organization.

Well-intentioned change can be made by force—by laying down the law—by saying, "This is how it's going to be around here." And the climate will soon be raw with anger and distrust. More helpful and effective change occurs when members of a parish can be led to see the general wisdom of a pastor's recommendations. The first tools are love, warmth, patience, and forgiveness—the tools Jesus used. We see moments of his impatience, but usually he was amazingly patient. He moved his constituency forward by means of a challenging love relationship that would not let them go.

In your first parish you have a wonderful chance to learn how to use the basic tools for ministry creatively, in spite of the inevitable odds. In this stage you will develop lifelong basic styles of ministry. Here, for example, is where you begin either to "do for" people or to "enable." Left unbothered, the vast majority of church members would always be simply consumers of the religious product, rather than producers of it. We play into their hands when we embrace a style of ministry in which we do everything for everybody. We teach all the adult classes, rather than developing leadership within the congregation. We lead the singing rather than have someone in the congregation do it. Encouraging parishioners to be creative leaders, serving in responsible roles, builds a congregation's inner life and equips it to serve Christ's mission more substantially.

Do we lead or do we follow? The minister who asks, "What does the congregation want to do?" and chiefly supports those preferences may be following rather than leading. Sometimes that style is right. For example, in small churches where there is typically a much larger sense of congregational ownership, the new pastor who is slow to put a strong hand on the rope that pulls the congregation along will often demonstrate strong leadership later. But in large churches there is a much higher expectation that the new pastor will take hold with bold moves early on. In any case, it is well to be prepared, be willing to offer proposals when they are needed and otherwise appropriate. And a good pastor in even a small church must be sure that the leadership role is not simply being avoided. A congregation's own instincts should never be ignored. They are important. But generally speaking, parishes benefit from direction suggested by a brave, visionary, loving leader.

Do we challenge people to tithe? Many ministers are afraid of money issues; they preach stewardship sermons in which people can hardly recognize that they are being asked to give. (To be sure, some pastors preach that way in order to protect their own purses—they themselves do not feel a commitment to significant financial investment in the mission of the church.) The best way for pastors to obtain a tithing congregation is to tithe themselves, and to let it be known that they do—without bragging.

There are many other development-of-style issues. Do we suggest closeness to the parishioners by saying, "Please stay away from my study until noon"? We've a great deal to learn in Stage One of parish life.

The Tension Between Personal Life and Career

This first stage will set the patterns for maintaining a balance between work and the stewardship of one's own personal health and relationships. This is a major issue for the pastor, the congregation, and the pastor's family, if there is one.

Mark Twain said that sometimes swearing provides a relief denied even to prayer! Jane, a clergy wife, does not call upon that form of relief except in those very private deep-in-the-parsonage moments when she is hurt and angry. She tells her husband he gives more attention to his work than he does to his wife and family. He denies it. But he can always carve out more time for the parish, though he can't find time to go to the park with the very family he insists he loves "more than anything."

Marge suffers the other side of the problem. Her minister husband moves more slowly than cold oil when it comes to church work. He'd rather play with the kids than go to work. He wants to fix supper. Marge loves his household participation, but she knows there is anger in the congregation because their minister doesn't seem involved in his work, and she scurries about the church, doing much of that work for him. She is worn out, and the congregation is embarrassed for her.

Those were real cases. Any minister who emphasizes personal life to the exclusion of the parish will be using the moving van a lot. And the minister who subordinates personal life to career is asking for an angry family and a possible divorce. Every minister, even if unknowingly, makes a decision regarding this tension. Each one needs to think this out and make clear decisions about ways to keep private life separate from career. Both are important, but lines must be drawn.

Each week contains twenty-one mods. Both a morning and an afternoon are mods. Let each of those mods represent four honest hours. An evening is a mod; let it represent two to three hours. We can be pretty careless about what we call work. For me, work includes anything—meetings and the writing of letters, for example—that is clearly intended for the parish or for the ministry. It includes the lunch hour only if I stay to work at my desk, or if I am truly engaged in business—not if it is a chatty break from the day with a colleague or friend.

I am convinced that ministers need to take great care to be fully engaged in their professional work for thirteen mods per week—generally no less and no more. Then save the remaining eight for purely personal time. It is tough to set appropriate limits for work and leisure, but it can be done. The minister must decide on those limits. Although the typical pastor puts in approximately fifty-five hours of on-duty time each week, it is appropriate to consider a forty-eight-hour work week as a fair minimum. Think in terms of mods or hours, but put in an honest week of work.

Of course, some clergy cannot honestly claim that they put in a full week of work. They cover up by suggesting that some of their chief pleasures are really work (writing a play, reading a novel, etc.). And some suggest that half a mod is a fair mod of work, but that is not usually so. A real sore point with lay people is that to clergy, evening meetings are work, while lay people work all day and then, in addition, must attend evening or weekend meetings. This is a difficult issue, because those meetings are in fact part of the minister's work. The minister often attends night after night of meetings, while that is not true of many lay people.

Here is a good way to deal with this issue: (1) resist complaining or drawing attention to the overload created by the evening meetings; (2) work hard during ordinary office hours—without drawing attention, but simply letting people notice; and (3) be kind but firm about the meetings you may miss, but give a fair reason—"I promised my son I'd attend his piano recital that night, and I need to keep that promise or he'd feel crushed." Sometimes it is fair to simply say, without tones of martyrdom or sarcasm, "I'd like to attend that meeting, but that's my day off. I know you need your free time, too, and I have discovered that if I don't protect my Mondays, my family soon gets shorted out of all my time."

People understand that—if they know that otherwise, you are putting in full hours and are generally available. Parishioners recognize high productivity on the part of their pastors. Quite frankly, some ministers can do six times the amount of work that others can in a unit of time. Some of that has to do with personality; some has to do with commitment. And some of it can be developed by a well-intentioned worker.

Then of course, many ministers convince themselves that they cannot get everything done in thirteen full mods, or only fifty to sixty hours, so they "must" work longer and later. It is easy to fall into that trap. In chapter four, my co-author writes helpfully about the importance of family happiness. There is a sad song sung by older, wiser professionals: "I wish I had taken more time for my family. That was my biggest mistake!" I heard one older pastor speak those very lines, and he clearly meant it. His glazed eyes pondered his coffee cup without seeing it, focusing on scenes of personal loss. Those of us present were silent. We knew the rest. Paragraphs went unsaid, but the long pause was eloquent. That man's children now lived lives contrary to his entire ministry. They had scarcely had any kind of meaningful relationship with their father. We listeners pondered our own records.

The son of another pastor expressed his long-held anger toward his "successful" father: "I was a star athlete in school. Not once did my dad come to see me win. He was always too busy at the church, caring about God's people, to care about me. I've hated him, the church, and God ever since." A short time later that pastor-father, not knowing that his son was seeing me for counseling, stopped in for a visit. He wondered if I had any clue as to why his son, my parishioner, seemed so distant. He was depressed about whatever had gone wrong between him and his only son.

Caring for our personal life and for our family, if we have family, is also a calling. But it requires a decision—not just one decision, to faithfully take every Monday and every Friday night off, for example—but repeated decisions, as your calendar is created every day. Someone phones and needs you at a meeting next Tuesday afternoon. But that is the time your daughter hopes you can be at her track meet. Any parent who doesn't opt for the track meet at least 75 percent of the time had better practice the melody to that sad song that begins, "I should have taken more time . . . ."

All this is to suggest that the first order of business for balance between the personal and the vocational is to give the "employer" what the pay check is intended to cover, and more, while also giving fair time and attention to rest and the re-creation of one's spirit and to one's personal relationships. This applies to singles as well as those who are married. It has Genesis 2:1-4a for support.

Single clergy who don't date need to have some close friends. Everyone needs a few intimates with whom one can be "real," can let it all out for the release of tension, can laugh to relieve the pressure. In every case, choose friends who can hold confidences and will not use their closeness to the minister for leverage in the congregation.

Single ministers who do date need to decide whether to date members of their church. This is somewhat like the matter of whether to allow personal friendships within the congregation—an issue any pastor faces. It is appropriate to seek personal nurture and friendship from people of the parish, and this can include courtship. It is natural to develop relationships among the people with whom one spends time. Indeed, lay people often are advised to join a church as a way to find friends, and that natural avenue must not be forbidden to pastors. It does, however, require sensitivity to the feelings of those parishioners who might feel excluded from others' special relationship with the pastor. The principle here is to show interest and concern to everyone without favoring one's pals. As for dating, many parents out there wish very much that their unmarried child could meet "that fine young minister." It can get complicated, but life is like that, and nurturing relationships must be allowed.

As more mothers become ministers—or ministers become mothers—there are added complications. The need to be available to family is both easier and more difficult for female clergy—easier, in that there remains a degree of cultural expectation that a woman must care for her children; more difficult, in that she must squeeze in the mothering in a way that is acceptable both to her own parenting instincts and to those who are watching and want their pastor to be a model parent, but still be a pastor "worth her salt." That's a lot to ask! The mother-pastor is not as tied to eight-to-five hours as the business-world mother. She has some flex in her schedule that helps when little Jodie is ill. And if the parishioners love her, that mother-pastor is allowed a great deal of freedom by the congregation.

On the other hand, she probably also has longer and stranger hours than do her sisters in other lines of work. She is on call around the clock. There are evening meetings, and the weekends are a zoo—weddings, services, youth group, and so on. Her free time is out of sync with her children's out-of-school time.

As a male pastor with children, when I was called in the middle of the night to rush to the emergency room, I slipped on my garb and got underway. My wife was home with the children. Had I been an unmarried parent, it would have been quite a problem. And many pastors now face that problem.

Our female colleagues have many issues to address, and no one can propose a sufficient list of solutions. However, one basic is that pastors who are also parents must be good parents first and foremost. It is a high calling to which Christ beckons each and every man and woman to whom is given the gift of a child. Balance and sensitivity are required, as in most things.

Some pastors are married to pastors. The clergy couple is a

phenomenon that requires a well-thought-out career design. Much must go right, and much can go wrong. I know one clergy couple with children who share the pastoral load of a church. The congregation assumes that the father is free from child care—that the mother-pastor cares for the children. People change those cultural images slowly. They want their church and their pastors to carry out the values they perceive to be traditional. Add to that the extra hurdle of not yet knowing how to cope with a mother who has a seminary degree framed and hanging above the washer-dryer in the manse. It requires a whole new way of thinking.

In the smaller communities, where so many clergy find themselves in their earliest years, these couples may very well be the first highly visible role models for new patterns of parenting. And they may see this as an opportunity for Christian mission in a new day. Clergy couples who clearly love each other, their children, and their parishioners, can demonstrate some important new ideas. They can teach by parenting in a truly caring, sharing way. The key to good parenting is love for each other and for the children. The key to success with a congregation is love for the people of the parish—even when those people are puzzled and doubtful. Given a transaction of affection between parish and pastors—the pace being set by the pastors—the community will accept these new arrangements and begin to adjust. Love is the most powerful force for opening minds and softening hearts.

Clergy couples face many other complications. Wanda says her Lutheran parishioners call her Wanda, but they call her husband Pastor! It is best not to make war over that kind of thing. The predicament could be explained to the officers, and maybe even to the congregation, asking for helpful equal treatment. But finally, the greatest difference probably will be made when, over a period of time, the congregation observes that both pastors do very good work. One of the more effective agents for change of attitude is good experience.

One clergy couple learned to obtain separate contracts when sharing any percentage of the pastoral load. When they had accepted a contract to serve one church together, that contract covered them both. They and the officers assumed that everything would work itself out. It didn't. That hard-won education taught them to advise each couple going to a shared pastorate to sign separate contracts, stating what portion of the full pastoral load each assumes, how much each will be paid, and what areas of work each will manage.

These are arduous definitions to draw up, of course. One could be stated as "approximately 60 percent of the 1⅓ position," for example, going on to indicate, "which shall translate into approximately 38 hours per week, normally including these responsibilities: _____." Then keep faith with the contract!

Another couple struggles with the awareness that people like to come to church on the Sundays Marna is preaching, but only the four back pews need to be dusted the Saturday before Mack is to preach. Mack notices. It is tough on his ego, and it affects her, too. It comes between them. Every marriage is tested in many ways, and each needs much commitment. The clergy couple, like any couple committed to marriage, will find means to resolve their struggles in ways that help both partners. In this particular "she's-a-better-preacher" case, it may mean that a loving husband must swallow the lump in his throat and decide to rejoice with his wife, to take the Apostle Paul at his word when he tells us there are differing gifts, and to learn better preaching methods from Marna. Then ask her to preach more often, if she is willing. Love her for it. Be grateful that she has the gift. It's called absolute grace!

Then there is Jack, a United Methodist pastor, whose wife, Kit, is pastor of a Presbyterian church across the street. They have all the usual problems, plus this added one—when Jack is out of town, his parishioners phone Kit with their questions, assuming that she'll take care of them. She is a minister, after all. What they don't remember is that she is not *their* pastor. And the same thing happens in reverse.

Kit and Jack need to be *very* committed to the principle of not trading stories about his and her members. Indeed, most clergy couples must deal with the degree of shop talk they will allow at home. One couple reports that they have agreed not to talk more than five minutes about church when they are at home or at leisure. These two just do not talk about work unless they are "on the clock."

And then, of course, the clergy couples who wonder how they'll manage to pull off succeeding calls or appointments in concert are legion. What if one gets a nibble before the other wants to move? Who will be willing to follow whom? Sometimes the money offered decides that problem. Sometimes divorce decides it. Sometimes the hope for other income decides it. Sometimes a pregnancy decides it. Sometimes nothing decides it easily. The important word is *commitment*—to each other . . . to love . . . to mutual support in marriage as well as service.

Decisions made casually or unwisely will bring a great deal of pain. Count on it. Decisions made carefully will still bring pain along the way, but there will be more joy in both parsonage and parish than there otherwise would have been. Count on it.

Some Very Private and Powerful Decisions

We must decide on our own about a few other issues that affect lifelong ministry. Most parishioners will never mention these things, because they think, rightfully, that we ought to know without being told. At the beginning of our ministry, we must make some personal agreements with God and with ourselves. These are the classic time bombs that could blow up and destroy us and our loved ones:

1. *Sex.* Have sex with your spouse, only. No exceptions! Don't ever—don't *ever*, at any time, touch a child, youth, or adult of *either* sex in any way that could be misunderstood.

2. *Alcohol/Street Drugs.* Abstinence can work anywhere, if practiced without judgment or prudishness. No congregation can cope with a pastor who uses street drugs, even if only occasionally. Some congregations can cope with modest use of alcohol, but even then, more than one or two rounds in any one mod of a day (such as afternoon or evening) will cause trouble—even though you are certain your body can handle it.

3. *Money.* The minister who does not tithe but asks a congregation to tithe will be seen as a phony. And the minister who gets into trouble with creditors will become known for it. As Achen in Joshua 7 found out, the wages of sin is publicity! The congregation will be embarrassed in the community and try to get rid of the offending minister. Learn to manage your money. Ask a trusted friend, parishioner, or colleague to help, if necessary.

4. *Power.* This is the slickest temptation of all. The minister is handed a generous portion of power and authority upon arrival and is tempted to overuse it. If it is used lovingly and creatively, more will be heaped upon the first helping. But if used dictatorially or wastefully, it will be consumed quickly, without replenishment. Then you're dead! Decide to use power the way Jesus did—unselfishly, to serve others.

That first stage of ministry—the post-seminary period—is critical . . . or, as one of my children used to say, awesome!

II

Beyond the First Parish

Some parents have jokingly commented that they should have the privilege of giving back their first child—that first one is only for practice. And some people in their second marriage insist that the second time around is the wonderful one. The assumption is that parents and marriage partners now know how to play the game. They're well warmed up for the pressures and pleasures of the adventure.

Similar things have been said of second and succeeding pastorates. Some small churches feel that they are practice fields for young ministers who look longingly toward the bigger leagues. Indeed, some of those wonderful small churches see that as part of their mission. They are not offended by the reality of the situation. Other congregations, of course, feel put off by the parade of "young squirt" preachers who come and go; who, during their thirty or so months, know all the answers and keep the congregation off-balance. In many cases both congregation and pastor sense great relief as the latter moves on to the next parish.

The second time around in parish work offers both hope and dilemma. Not every parent fumbles the first child. Sometimes that child is loved, nurtured, and led into life very well. On the other hand, some parents repeat with their second and third children every mistake they made with the first. They have learned nothing. And one has the feeling that some people are faking their broad smiles as they profess their Camelot in marriage No. 2. Many have never examined their earlier experiences in ways that will lead them to build on the better parts of the past and change what needs changing. They duplicate all the bad habits of the previous experiences.

The Hope

In some way or other, everyone needs to make changes and new starts. Those who feel they have never brought some disaster to colleagues or constituencies must have a powerful denial system, or perhaps they just do not recognize failure. Most of us can look back with embarrassment at things said, things unsaid, things done, missed opportunities for ministry.

Some people feel hopeful when they can move from the practice field to a new field where the profession can be performed more wisely. Mistakes in the first parish do not need to force closure, although sometimes this happens. There may be instances of serious moral failure, which, though they may not force us out of the ministry, do make pastoring in the present community impossible. In such cases a clean slate in a new community is helpful and hopeful. Sometimes the managerial style of a pastor is so objectionable to the people of the parish that, right or wrong, the emotional blockage is too locked in to budge. And many times the mismatch is that of a very good congregation and a very good pastor, but they are not right for each other. There are also mismatches of gifts and expectations. In all these cases, a change might be helpful.

For some pastors, the hope is that the children and the family may be better off in another school system or another set of community conditions. If a move is in a direction the pastor perceives to be a career improvement, then it feels good to be progressing forward and "upward." Maybe it's closer to the "home office," or to a preferred part of the country, or toward other career goals. Often the only thing better in the new location is the salary or the pastor's residence. Those things can be pretty important. While some smaller congregations offer fair salaries and, in some cases, excellent residences, many others want top-quality ministry for bargain-basement salaries and have not made a significant improvement in the minister's house in years. A move may help.

The Examination

One minister did something that would not work for everyone. As he was about to leave his first parish, he drew up a simple questionnaire which he gave to the members of the congregation, asking them to fill it out and return it unsigned. Basically, he asked, "What things about my ministry here have been the most helpful?" and, "Recognizing that no one can do all things well, but that I hope to improve throughout my ministry, kindly help me by telling me what things could have been better." He received one or two responses from unhappy members, but there were also many warm affirmations and thoughtful suggestions.

Cancer-prevention groups have a tough time getting people to perform self-examination. Many of us are either too fearful of what we might discover, too certain that all is well, or we just simply do not get around to finding the time for it.

Someone has said that the unexamined life is a meaningless life. It is scary and difficult, but it is important that all pastors frequently examine their life and work. Good prayer and meditation include self-examination. Jesus often took time out for R and R—rest and recreation. Re-creation or renewal requires a good look at what we are doing. It requires dealing with the following questions: Could I be doing this a better way? Is this working? What needs to change, or what needs to happen? What did I do right, and what did I do poorly? Are there needs that are not being met? Do I have a practice or a personality trait that gets in the way of my work or my own well-being? If so, how can I begin to work on that? Whose help do I need? Do I have something as ordinary as a facial or verbal tic that gets in the way of good communication?

One of the real dangers is that we can easily fall into the habit of "file drawer" ministry. After inventing certain programs and practices, pastors can simply pull out the memory of the way they did a certain thing before, and repeat it again and again. A wise pastor asks whether a certain practice really did work well enough to be resurrected. That suggestion applies in the first parish, too, of course, but the larger danger is that the succeeding parishes are not really new pastorates. Rather, the pastors simply repeat the first parish over and over in different locations. People do survive that way, but they are not effective.

The self-examination serves not only to weed out weak ideas and poor programs from the ministry tool kit. Often the analysis is performed to be sure that even good sharp tools are really the right ones for the new job. For example, during my first pastorate I developed a superb confirmation-education plan, complete with comprehensive student books, extensive weekly lesson plans for the leader, suggested audio visuals, and so on. It was so perfect that it was borrowed by colleagues for use in their own churches.

So when I moved to my second parish, there was no question about what I would use for confirmation education. But that "perfect" plan I had developed in my previous location flopped. The problem was not that I had attempted to repeat a bad practice. I was reusing a very sharp tool that had done a good job. But even the good things cannot always be the right ones in another place. "Ya gotta' know the territory!" as the sales reps sang in *Music Man*. Ya gotta' know yourself, too, and this requires frank and frequent self-examination. If it doesn't happen during the first pastorate, it surely must happen as we move from parish to parish, or we are doomed to repetitious mediocrity.

The Realities of Succeeding Parishes

The person who first said that we are never too old to learn must be very, very old by now. If still living, however, it is a pretty good bet that that person is still learning. I am more than 70 percent into the typical forty-year career run, and I am still learning. One great rush of learning occurred as I became deeply involved in the work of my second pastorate.

It is with a little embarrassment that I recall thinking, in my first parish, that I could not imagine being any busier. I thought about the "big boys" in the big city churches—as impressively busy as they appeared, I was surely just as busy. Perhaps even busier. I enjoyed thinking that way. I was a good audience for my own fantasies.

Then came a new pastorate, and a lesson lay waiting in the bushes to grab me. I found out what busy was. But the long, hard work of my first parish was good preparation for the longer hours and harder work in the next pastorates.

Then as I got into my middle years and edging beyond, that extra workload had to be taken care of on slightly but steadily decreasing levels of energy. Greater attention had to be paid to work limits. I had to find a way to work fewer evenings without cheating the parish. My day off became even more important than before. It became necessary to pay closer attention to good stewardship of the body. Good-news reports on my annual physicals became my wife's favorite birthday present!

It follows, of course, that in second and succeeding parishes, we ministers need to become better managers of the time we give to the work of the church. Whereas earlier we attended every district committee meeting we could— partly for fellowship, partly to be a company-person, partly to learn the ropes in the system—we now discover we must be much more selective. We attend only those meetings that are clearly necessary for some reason or other.

Ben and Sue are a clergy couple in their second shared-position pastorate, 125 miles from where most of their denomination's meetings are held. They have a simple rule of thumb. They will not normally attend any meeting that does not last at least as long as it takes to travel to the meeting and back again. They will not drive four hours for a forty-five minute meeting unless it has a critical content, or unless they have an unusually large dose of the need to see colleague friends.

As we move into larger and more complex congregations, we need to be more discriminating about many projects and practices that consume time and energy. The pressure to get more things done and to see more people increases. And another significant pressure applies—the pressure to do better quality work.

As we move along, and especially as we move "up," there is an increasing expectation on the part of congregations that ministers will preach sermons of substance, with oratorical skill. It is much harder to just get by. This is even more true in larger communities where there are more options for church-going people. Potential members have choices, and present members can move to another church with much greater ease than in a small town, where everybody knows everybody and talks about any major move a citizen makes.

So if we move into churches that are going to "go" anywhere, we must deliver. The pressure is on. Officers expect much more sophisticated programs and extensive financial reports. They expect efficient operation of the church and chairing of meetings. There is an expectation of higher quality work in almost every way.

Perhaps there is a lower expectation in one way only. Larger churches in larger communities, into which ministers may begin to move in mid-career, often expect less home visitation. Indeed, in these later pastorates, it may be impossible to accomplish much home visitation at all after the initial round of getting-to-know-the-parish visits. A major change many of us experience in these parishes is that we have fewer one-on-one contacts with people, especially in larger churches. Much more contact happens in groups. In my first parish there were few groups within the congregation's program life; there was much more need and opportunity to see individuals in homes and in stores and on the street. Group contact can be just as valuable, but it certainly is different. It requires attention.

For many ministers, the nature of meeting parishioners is unlike the way they may have done it in the early stages of their profession. In my own mid-life pastoral era, I make approximately four hundred personal contacts each week with members of a seven-hundred-member congregation. That figure does not include all those present in the worship services (typically 550 per Sunday). There is a way to conduct worship, however, that can make the experience seem quite personal. In a service that effectively connects with the congregation, many members of a parish feel personally touched or in touch with their pastor.

Still, my four-hundred-some weekly contacts with parishioners are personal, in that I speak to each person. I am dealing with each one individually. These contacts are not in the home, and rarely in the supermarket, but usually occur in and around the church's program life—as people gather for church functions, in personal counseling, and in relation to other personal or church needs. Most are of necessity brief, but no less personal or well meant. Such contacts must be real, even if momentary. If we fake them in order to make the numbers come out right, we will be seen as manipulative.

I cannot speak with every worshiper as the crowd leaves, because it is impossible to stand at all exits at once. But I stand at the main exit to take the hand and speak with each person who goes my way. I ask Mabel if her husband is feeling better. I ask Bud if his daughter has found a job yet. I wish Valarie a happy birthday (I study the birthday book every Sunday morning for that day and the next six days—people love to have us remember their birthdays). If Phil has his parents with him and I've met them before, I put my internal computer to work, pull up one detail, and go with it. Even if I do not remember their names, I may remember that they are

47

from Iowa. So I will say, "Well, how's everything in Iowa?" Take a little girl's hand, tell her how pretty her dress is, and her admiring parents have somehow been hugged. Those things touch people. It is personal contact. The minister who genuinely loves people can do those things naturally and with integrity. It is pastoral.

I do not wait until after the worship service to meet and greet all those great people who come to worship. From the first moment they begin to enter, I stand in the arrival area to meet and mix with them, up until the very moment I must begin the service, being careful to extricate myself from the longer conversations. My purpose is to touch base—but not with just one or two. It is a rich time for preacher and people to make contact. I teach an adult Sunday school class, but at least once each month I arrive a few minutes late. On that morning, I walk through all the children's classrooms to greet the children and once more thank the teachers for teaching. Those are personal contacts that have real meaning.

When the parent of a member of the parish dies, I send a carefully written letter. The same letter is sent to everyone; I don't hide that fact. I do not have time to write a great three-page letter at every death. Instead, I spent one whole day writing and rewriting, then stored in the computer, that one basic letter. It deals with feelings and gives examples of personal experiences of loss. I've created a similar letter to send to parishioners who have lost a sibling and another for colleagues who have lost loved ones. Those letters work as well as, and sometimes better than a visit in the home. The recipient doesn't need to dust the house for it, and the letter is reread and passed on to other relatives. It is a very personal thing. Usually some member of the family tells me that the letter was read by everyone in the family and they all felt helped by it. A whole family can be embraced that way.

Some deaths, such as that of a child or a young parent, affect feelings for a lifetime. I keep a tickler file of such deaths, because it is certain that when those heavy days come around each year, the family will think of its loss. On the first anniversary, I phone or stop in just to say that I remember, too. Each year after that, I send a small note: "I'm thinking of you today as I remember Jill's death. I hope you are okay." We don't need to worry about reminding the bereaved of their pain. It is already there. For us to ignore it is the greater danger.

A couple of days after parishioners get home from the hospital, they may receive a phone call from me to see how they are feeling. When a circle meets in the church, I make sure I leave my office to drop in and say hello. It is best to do this about dessert time so there can be a bit of chit-chat with individuals without interrupting a group discussion.

Those are just examples, some of which might or might not be helpful for other pastors, but it would be difficult to find a congregation for which those kinds of things would not work. The personality and operational style of the minister are critical, however, and the examples require a naturally gregarious person—or one who is willing to honestly attempt the sociability that congregations want. Many ministers are less able to relate naturally and lovingly than their parishioners hope. Even so, most congregations will go a long way with the more solitarily inclined minister who asks for help.

Such a pastor could preach a sermon on the power of love and the nurturing effect of caring relationships. In that sermon the loner could simply and straightforwardly say, "I myself do not find it easy to make small talk, mix and visit, or relate in the ways I know would help people. But I want to be more sociable. Will you help me by forgiving my attempts that seem clumsy or obvious—realize that I am really trying? Help me by being patient when I fail, become scared, and retreat once more to my books in the study. Help me by taking the initiative even when you think that I as the minister should take the initiative. Help me by praying for me in this attempt to be a better pastor. Maybe we can all help each other." That kind of honesty and vulnerability will give integrity to what will sometimes be a feigned way of dealing with people.

We must be committed to a style of ministry which recognizes that in the end—and in the beginning—people are infinitely more important that ideas, plans, books, or any sermon. Jesus was extraordinarily available to people. His attitude is a good model. One quick clue for most ministers is a glance at our office. (Toes will be stepped on here, but this matter is crucial to the effectiveness of parish work.)

If you find a pastor's office where most surfaces are covered with hundreds of books, documents, filmstrips, and periodicals, it is very likely the office of a pastor who probably doesn't want to visit. Stuff may need to be cleared off of a chair in order for you to stay. That office is unconsciously arranged more for content and concepts than for people, and that pastor's whole life may well be the same way.

Then look into a minister's office which has an arrangement of comfortable chairs positioned for conversation, always ready for people, and you probably are looking into the office of a people person. That pastor has designed the office for people and probably will come out from behind the desk to sit in the conversation circle with you. None of this is absolute, but it is one measure that often comes pretty close.

All these comments are intended to indicate that there are ways and means to effect the contact between pastor and parishioners which is essential to productive pastoral work. That is important at this point because alternatives to personal visitation in homes become a necessity in many of our mid-career pastorates. Pastors who move from early-stage parishes, however, recognize that they give up something wholesome and potentially gratifying when those home visit contacts can no longer be part of the pastoral pattern.

Another more encouraging change begins to show itself as we enter second-stage parishes: We become more credible. Assuming that we generally make sense, dress so as not to offend our constituency, clearly like people, seem to speak the truth, and practice the profession with integrity, we begin to notice that we get a better hearing when we say what we think. No longer are we the twenty-five-year-old graduates telling the town banker what life is all about, while the banker sits there looking doubtful. We are men and women of some experience, saying things that seem to ring true to all kinds of people. Graying hair helps, as well as other indications of maturity and seasoning. The words are rarely if ever spoken, but one can feel the attitude: "This person speaks with authority." This is one good part of a generally wonderful stage of pastoral life.

There are more tools in the tool kit, and now we know more about how to use them. We know which ones work best for particular tasks. We will have more work to do, but our confidence is more believable, and we can produce a better product. It can be a very good time.

III

The Forks in the Road

Ponder the ministers who stand at some point in their career and say, "Golly! Where do I go from here? Which route do I take now?" They face a fork in the career path, and it can happen at almost any time. It can happen several times. But when it happens, they enter a new stage of pastoral and career life, at least to some degree.

Sometimes this new stage is greeted with excitement and joy. Then again, sometimes one lies awake at night, wondering what to do. It can be a real struggle! So much depends on the decision.

You may face such a fork for the first time when you decide whether you should move toward a career as a generalist in ministry, or as a specialist. And if as a specialist, then in what specialty? Can one go back to the fork in the road and take another direction later, if the first dead ends?

Few "fork" decisions need to be life-lasting. But they are life-impacting. Prayer, thought, and study are needed.

The Generalist

Solo pastors are generalists. Like the old family physicians, they are engaged in the general practice of ministry. And, as in the case of physicians, that's what almost all ministers were engaged in until recent decades. One was a generalist for the entire career. Options were seldom considered, since few were available. One of those few options was a career as a missionary.

Today the structures of society have changed, requiring adjustment in the methods of every professional group. Though more complicated than can be covered here, to state it simply, people have gathered into larger institutional groups—larger schools, larger malls, larger companies. There has been a notable transfer of population from smaller communities to larger communities and from smaller congregations to larger congregations. Many smaller congregations and communities have actually disappeared.

Though it is true that churches in America now number 75 percent more than in the first decade of this century, and many of those are in small communities, there are fewer congregations in many of the traditional denominations. In my state, 15 percent fewer congregations of my denomination exist now than five decades ago. That represents quite a number.

Still, in spite of the movement to larger groups, the majority of congregations are still under two-hundred members in almost every denomination. These thousands of congregations needing pastoral leadership require solo pastors, and this will be true for a long time. Some pastors are made for that type of work; others don't feel cut out for it and feel trapped in it.

There probably always will be work for ministers who choose general practice, but it may require adjustment to several realities—smaller congregations, smaller towns, multiparish arrangements, and so on. It may mean greater use of the bivocational minister and perhaps smaller salaries.

Whether or not it is fair, the fact remains that ministers who spend their lives as solo pastors of small congregations receive less income through the years than do senior pastors in large churches. And their pension checks will be smaller. Typically, though not always, their expenses also are smaller, but not enough to offset the salary disparity. It is a fact of life that will not change in most denominations.

Some pastors do not mind the salary difference; others are deeply frustrated. Some prefer a simpler life-style; others yearn for the finer things, angry (either consciously or subconsciously) that they live a Chevrolet life while other ministers wave at them from Oldsmobiles. Some talk of vacations at Aunt Angie's; others talk of their most recent trip to London. There is a price to be paid for some career choices. Of course, sometimes it is not a matter of choice, but how one is assigned by the hierarchy. Or it may have something to do with competency or other limiting factors. For some, this issue is a real and meaningful element in the sense of God's call to ministry.

Size of community, congregation, and salary are not the only factors in one's decision about career direction, but they do have impact. The impact may be on the ministers' feeling level, or it may affect a spouse or family. Many of us like to think amount of income should be beside the point; yet, the price tag of ministry is part of the mix when making fork-in-the-road decisions.

Solo pastoral work is wonderful for those who care neither to manage nor to be managed. The typical solo pastor works hard and for many hours. However, such a pastor has a high degree of flexibility and usually can control the schedule. Relatives of pastors sometimes misunderstand the minister's life. They may visit in the home for a few days and be impressed by how much free time the minister has, not understanding that the moment the guests leave, that same minister rushes out to catch up on hospital calls, desk work, and meetings. It is quite a privilege to have such schedule-flex. Solo pastoring is excellent for those who enjoy that freedom and can handle it responsibly.

Solo work is also helpful to those pastors who are loners. Some ministers just don't feel they are team people. They don't dislike people—they just prefer to work alone for the most part. Many do great work in single-person canoes; they just don't fit as part of a rowing team. Studies do indicate that while congregations have a strong preference for ministers who are caring extroverts, education in theology tends to attract loners and introverted personality types. That contradiction presents many difficulties in parish life. If ministers prefer solitude to the point of an inability to develop a caring relationship with the members of the parish and community, they might consider a specialty which requires a lesser degree of human contact, such as writing, teaching, or research.

Not all solo pastoring is in smaller towns, of course, but one outstanding pastor in the Midwest is determined to spend his ordained life in small congregations in small towns, because that is exactly where he feels God has called him to serve. He loves small-town life. He cherishes the chatter of down-home folks. He thrives on the food at potluck dinners. He knows each family personally, in a way that he can pass on God's love. He lingers at the postoffice each morning, knowing that in an hour's time, most of the citizens of the community will come by. He enjoys being his own boss without bossing others or having co-workers leaning over his shoulder. A part-time secretary in each parish he serves is just right.

This pastor feels fulfilled by preaching every Sunday. He is nurtured by frequent visitation. He is happy about an involvement in Christian education that doesn't take up the whole week every week. He enjoys the scaled-down nonexhausting events of a more modest-sized youth group. Several churches have been blessed by the ministry of this dedicated man. He is a general practitioner, and he wouldn't have it any other way!

Later changes in direction are possible, though in many denominational systems it is difficult to spring from solo work to an executive position. Most governing bodies in search of executive types tend to prefer candidates who have had experience supervising sizable staff. However, movement to other specialties is usually possible. Ministers in solo work who depend on the call system seem to make their move to larger congregations before age fifty-five. Upward movement after that age is more likely for those known to have exceptional talents, particularly as preachers.

But the general practice of ministry is the direction of choice for many, possibly most, ministers. One pastor, after having been in a specialized form of ministry for a few years, returned to parish work. He commented, "I believe the gospel is experienced best 'on location.' "

A Specialty: The Senior Pastor

Jesus amazes me! He had twelve associate pastors! At one time, there was some squabbling about who would have preferred status, and one was fired—or rather, the termination was managed in a way that allowed a resignation. Then a search committee selected a new associate, who got the job but seemingly never really made it. At least, his installation service was about the last we heard of him. And Jesus had to spend major blocks of time teaching his staff the attitudes he had in mind and the way he wanted things done.

I often think about that. How did he do it?! One might think his staff would have strung him up—but no, others did that, with a little help from one associate.

It seems to me that we senior pastors spend most of our time dealing with personnel situations. Nobody ever told me that in seminary! In fact, with only a few exceptions, such as in some Baptist systems, seminaries do not prepare ministers to be senior pastors. We learn by watching, reading, and most of all, by doing. Younger turks in ministry enjoy the "ain't it awful" stories about senior pastors. I did the same when I was outside looking in. But now I know what it's like.

Ministers who set out to be senior pastors of multiple-staff congregations need to understand several things. For one thing, it helps to be a "first born"—the first child born to parents, or a person with the characteristics of a first-born child. Persons with these characteristics typically have become accustomed to being in charge. Those given to uncertainty, accommodation, or avoidance invite more grief than they may be able to bear. The larger salary won't be worth it.

Although senior pastors do not deal personally with all aspects of the church program, they do create, sustain, or complicate the climate, which then affects everything that happens. There is a big load on their whole being, every day. And it seems that few people understand the load, the tension, and the cost. The bigger the boat, the more critical that a captain be in charge—not an insensitive, dictatorial Captain Bly, but a definitely in-charge person. The captain must be able to say, "We need to go that way!" and have it understood, or terrible collisions are in the offing.

There will be attempts to take over the ship: Sometimes an associate will try to grab the wheel; sometimes an officer or a group of lay people feel the need to rescue the congregation from Dr. Too-Much-in-Charge. And sometimes these other people actually have more vision and energy than the pastor and do need to move forward.

The candidate for the senior pastor career should prepare to be a personnel manager. The president of a large corporation can afford a vice-president for personnel, but the head of staff in a church can't. It is time consuming, often difficult, and sometimes an assault on the feelings. There usually is support and guidance from a personnel committee, but it meets only once a month, and personnel issues don't wait for the fourth Tuesday at 7:30. Staff members become confused when the senior must take on the managerial role, which may require a firmness that conflicts with the Mr. Nice Guy image of the pastor. It's also confusing to the pastor, who must be a wonderful person while insisting that the work be done, be done well, and be done on time.

Nor does a committee do the administering. It sets policy and prepares budget. *You* are the administrator. You'll need to know the meaning of FICA, and FTE, and Form 1099, nonexempt employees, independent contractors, and sexual harassment—and those are the easy ones. It is involved, delicate work. And—get ready for this one—not all your staff will like you. Sometimes it is disappointing, and even painful. But it is true.

Then too, officers of a large church have a strong inclination to behave as if the church were small. A board of fifteen to thirty people can spend an hour or more worrying over whether the office should be open at noon. It is a rare corporation whose board of officers spends time on such management details. But church boards find it difficult to stick to broad policy setting, budget adoption and review, programmatic overview, and big-picture thinking. All this puts a tremendous strain on the head-of-staff pastor.

There are so many systems, programs, and people to be monitored in a large church, one needs to be an able and willing delegator, or one will fly apart, trying to cover too many bases. Those who are close with information should exempt themselves from this route to retirement. The senior pastor who plays the "congregational cards" close to the chest is inviting frustration levels that may result in destructive explosions. Other pastors on the staff, as well as other key workers, need to feel included in information about problems, plans, and so on.

Distance is created by so many common, to-be-expected conditions. A large congregation is amazingly complex. The larger and more complicated the church, the harder the head pastor must hold on to keep policies, guidelines, and practices in place. The daily pressures by new members and new officers to change the course could wreck the ship if someone strong is not in charge. But when senior pastors practice that leadership faithfully—not dictatorially—they will be seen as autocratic, unbending, unapproachable. They cannot say Yes to everybody all the time. When the answer is No, another inch of distance is generated, and one begins to learn about the ulcers of leadership.

To be the senior pastor in larger congregations takes talent and a generous share of guts. It is not for the timid, tired, or insecure. It is for those who are willing to live with great pressure. The proverbial buck really does stop at the desk of the senior pastor; the larger the congregation and the more complicated its program life, the more frequently and insistently that buck is slammed down on the desk.

There are few places to talk about these things without being accused of whining. Few friends understand, few parishioners understand, and few colleagues understand, unless, of course, they too are senior pastors of large, active congregations. It can be scary and lonely for the senior pastor. Loneliness is a real issue. Many senior pastors have said it is a loneliness they never knew in their previous years as associates or solo pastors. Being a senior pastor has provided me with more excitement *and* more loneliness than I could have imagined.

There are blessings in the senior position, however. Typically, one can reach such a career line and last in it only if one has some particularly useful talents and skills. It is good personally to be able to exercise those talents and skills where they have broader application than may be possible in a small congregation. If one has special organizational abilities, it is gratifying to be able to affect the structure in a large situation and see it run productively. Many churches would greatly benefit from such leadership.

If, as is often the case, a minister's skill is preaching, then it is satisfying to practice that vocation where many people can listen, learn, grow, and be moved to serve. It is a heady experience. And unless it is *only* a heady experience, it can serve Christ's church in powerful ways.

Generally speaking, senior pastors of large congregations know that they are taken seriously by the local community and by others. They are called upon as spokespersons for positions and causes—much more than when they were associates or solos. One effect is that senior pastors are given a much larger constituency than their own parish and are allowed opportunities for significant impact. They are quoted in newspapers, since they have greater access to community leaders and events. All parts of the community need the gospel, and God calls some of us to work among the leaders of the community.

Senior pastors get there by different routes. Some take small churches as solo pastors and the churches grow to become large multistaff congregations. The pastors learn their role in stages, as they solve one growing problem after another. Other pastors move into the whole new world of seniorship after a series of solo pastorates. Still others start in large churches as associates, so they already have some understanding of the role. But no route can adequately prepare someone for the role of senior pastor.

Those who consider this fork in their career need to be sure they can stand the inevitable pressure. They need to assess honestly whether they are sufficiently equipped and skilled to carry the burden. If they usually carry the pain of angry protest for days, or even hours after the event, they should ask if the sacrifice of health is worth the "glory." They need to have the capacity to relax. It is said of angels that they can fly because they take themselves lightly. Senior pastors are not angels, but they need to know how to take themselves and their roles both seriously and lightly.

Senior pastors also must have the social skills needed to mix and move with ease among all kinds of people. Those who cannot will suffer in the large pulpit position—and the church will suffer as well. This is a special calling in which only a few can serve comfortably, but it is one of the fields of mission in which God needs servants.

In addition to all the other needed qualities, I'll mention only one more: Senior pastors must be able to see the "big picture" and keep that larger image in view. The daily parade of little issues—"Pastor, how many sandwiches should we prepare for the lunch after the funeral tomorrow?"—can pull us too far down to the gritty detail. We need to respond to such things helpfully, but we also need to be able to move quickly back to the larger canvas. I call it Thinking Twenty.

I enjoy the detail and the interruptions that put me in

contact with people of the parish. And yet I push myself to go back to planning. I want that planning to be such that even a simple policy adopted today does not complicate the work of the congregation twenty or so years from now. There are many demands for now-oriented decisions, but decisions create waves which may affect the future of the mission of the parish. Senior pastors need to know how to hold to the long-haul directions and remain committed to them. This requires big thinking and ability to plan for the future, and those who see in themselves the characteristics described in this section should go forward with confidence and purpose.

A Specialty: The Career Associate

A bad thing almost happened when I almost became an associate pastor. That is not a comment on the position, but on myself. The fork in the road was right there in front of me. I had had a few years of solo pastoring, and two senior pastors asked me to be their associate. Both were ministers I admired, and each would have meant a move to an enticing city. And I had the skills to do the job.

Then a good thing happened. I prayed—and then I seemed led to talk with an older and wiser colleague. That man saved my ordained skin when he said, "You are not cut out to be an associate pastor! You'd hate it. You have creative urges in too many areas of ministry, so either work alone or as a leader of staff. It's okay. . . . God did it to you."

That was excellent advice and I heeded it. But it does not apply to everyone. To some equally valuable, God-gifted pastors, I'm sure that same wise pastor would have said, "Be an associate pastor. Your skills are spectacular in a few well-defined areas of ministry. You take direction admirably. God called you to be a servant, and for you that may mean serving on some good leader's staff."

I will simply use my first staff associate as a case in point. She was excellent. In my opinion, she has God-given attributes which may call her to a lifelong career as an associate pastor. For one thing, she is a second-born with second-born characteristics. This means, for instance, that she is skilled at accommodating without denying herself. There will be continual strife if two or more people exhibit first-born behavior.

My associate did not always agree with my decisions, but she knew how to work with them. She knew it was my job to make tough decisions, and she knew how to feed the thought processes without challenging my personhood or my role.

She had outstanding nurturing skills. An associate pastor needs to have an open ear—to listen like a good parent, who sooths the hurt of the children without necessarily agreeing with the complaints. When parishioners were angry at the senior pastor, the officers, the church, or something else, she listened creatively. She never pitted her natural following within the congregation against me or my natural following.

She understood that an associate pastor needs to keep the senior pastor informed. In brief, capsulized form, she would tell me almost daily the significant things that were going on in the groups, programs, and people. I was kept up on who was ill, who was getting better, who was changing jobs, who was angry, what group needed new leadership, where I could help, and so on. She really helped me to be a better senior pastor.

She was adept at taking initiative within the areas of her responsibility. She could quickly see my dreams or directions, and take them from there. She was courteous and care-full (as in *caring*) in pointing out her insights and suggestions as programs were shaped. It was teamwork.

So there we are. If an individual is a real team player and has the ability to work skillfully in particular areas of congregational life, but does not feel called to heavy overall responsibility and administrative detail, then he or she could serve Christ's Church fruitfully as a career associate. Such people would need to be at peace with the fact that salary checks will always be smaller than those handed to the senior pastor. The community and much of the congregation will always think of the church as being the senior pastor's. The senior pastor almost certainly will be the main parent figure, the one to whom lay leaders will look to see whether the proposal the associate suggests is okay. Accommodaters can cope with these realities. Those who cannot will want to take another direction.

Lesser Known Specialties

Some options, of which one seldom thinks, can work well for some pastors and some parishes. I know at least one mid-age pastor who reversed the typical direction. He gave up his senior pastor position and sought a solo pastorate in a small church in a town of fifteen hundred people. He reveled in the more relaxed atmosphere and the numerous one-on-one contacts. It was his new career.

And there is at least one minister who went to school to obtain a degree in music and became minister of music in a mid-sized congregation. His background in Bible, theology, and church work gave excellent support to his specialty. He had a new career.

One woman, a very competent and loved parish pastor, became a minister-at-large for the area conference of her denomination. Whether the congregation was large or small, if it was without pastoral leadership for a period of time, she filled in for the duration. She was still a pastor, and many people felt the power of her great ministry. It became her new career.

Several ministers have made mid-career decisions to do interim pastoral work, and chapter 5 contains some helpful suggestions for that option.

The "Out" Option

The signpost at a fork in the road always has a group of arrows listing the various ways to go. One arrow points to

"Out." That option is always open. It has its complications, but for some it offers hope.

For some clergy, the ministry was not so much their idea as the dream of their parents, the wish of a beloved pastor back home, or the desire of others. The full awareness of the reality did not penetrate until after a few years in the ministry. The role doesn't feel right, and it isn't right. The fit is unnatural. To such people, every task of ministry is difficult and dreary. Even if they have a high regard for the office of pastor, these particular ministers must get out to have peace and an opportunity for fulfillment.

Like church members, there are ministers who experience an honest change of faith or theological orientation. I know a Presbyterian minister who recently felt compelled to become a Mormon; a Covenant minister who is sure he now needs to become a Presbyterian. I know a Baptist minister who, although at one time he felt a deep faith in Jesus Christ, came to deny that belief. He was honest about it, and out of respect for believing Baptists, as well as for his internal integrity, he left the ministry and became a Unitarian layperson.

A few ministers want to make it work, but it just doesn't. Or they know now that they need to work where they don't need to hear all the bitter complaints church people can make. And there are other reasons.

Getting out of the ministry needs to remain an honorable option, of course, but it requires so many answers to so many questions. What can I do to make a living? How do my dependents feel? Can I make a move while I am still young enough to get interviews in other lines of work? Those are just a few of the most obvious.

The very image of the fork in the road implies a tough decision. My advice is to get good advice. It is true that we make our own decisions—no one can make them for us—but we help ourselves when we resist going only with our own instincts and desires. In the end, our instincts may be correct. They often are. But the wisest of us know that we don't know enough on their own.

Ask several trusted, knowledgeable people. Pump each one by asking as many questions as you can think of. Don't predetermine their answers by suggesting that you are really seeking affirmation of your wishes. And if you have a family, make sure that family is very much a part of those conversations.

Then proceed, knowing an old truth—God will be beside you, even on bumpy trails. And here is another truth—on almost all roads, there eventually is a place where you can safely turn around or change directions.

IV

The Best Years

Several years ago the serious cartoon strip "The Small Society" pictured a middle-aged couple sitting on a park bench.

The man is saying to the woman, "Hoo-boy. Whatever happened to the best that was yet to come, Shirley?"

She replies, "Maybe it was already—"

When it comes to determining the best years of one's ministry, we have to say that it is all very relative. Obviously, it is not possible to say what the best years are or should be for someone else. For some, there seem never to be any "best years." For others, those years may be at the beginning, or in the middle, or even at the very end. Perhaps most of us keep thinking that they are still to come. But when trying to put life in perspective, must we say that the best has already been?

One of my students at St. Paul School of Theology experienced his best years in his first pastorate. He was fifty years old and had entered seminary after a successful business career. At graduation, he knew he perhaps had not long to live, because of a serious heart ailment. But he seized the opportunities of his very first pastorate with the excitement and enthusiasm of a child who finds a shiny new bike under the Christmas tree. Into the next few years, that man poured his entire life, and then he died. Those, he said, were the best years of his life.

Others, fresh from school and pulsating with new learning and many bright ideas, find the going pretty rough. It is not flattering to an eager seminary graduate to discover that the first parish is not exactly expecting radical transformation. It is frustrating to experience what Jacques Barzun meant when he said, "You understand what a dynamo feels like when it is discharging into a non-conductor" (*Teacher in America*, p. 27). Such an experience is not the stuff of "best years."

I like to quote a favorite text from Jeremiah to younger ministers: "The Lord said, 'Jeremiah, if you get tired racing against men, how can you race against horses? If you can't even stand up in open country, how will you manage in the jungle by the Jordan?' " (12:5 TEV).

I fail to understand those who are inclined to consider the very first years as the best. Sometimes young ministers do fall into parishes that will accept and encourage them with grace and forbearance, pleased to have youthful ideas. But for someone to look back after thirty or forty years and declare that the first years were the best would seem to distort the concept of the ministry as a calling.

An old Spanish proverb declares that the road is always better than the inn. Along the long road there are surely many bumps and potholes and detours, but if one concentrates only on the "inn," the end, or even the beginning, much of the adventure and exhilaration will be missed. On the long road of ministry it is the accumulation and assimilation of experience that counts. As this fund of experience enlarges, deepens, and matures, one is building a durable foundation for the best years.

A former student of mine, Gene Winkler, with an established reputation as an effective pastor, suggests that after two decades, a deeper spiritual life results from a viable baggage of experience. As ministry endures, one learns how to handle surprises, learns how the church operates. He uses the analogy of tennis, in which continuing experience enables one to call the right shots.

Continuing experience occurs to us often without our planning for it, but it may be continuing *education*—something *we* seek and plan for—that assures the growing quality of ministry. The best years may well be measured as a long period of time, if one deliberately participates in continuing education. The crucial factor here is that the minister must be motivated to *seek* such programs. Many do not. Perhaps they perceive a choice between continuing education and vacation time, although such programs are *not* to be spent as vacation time, even if the minister often has difficulty convincing a parish committee that time must be granted for both. One might ask such a committee how they would like their physician or the teacher of their children never to bother with continuing education. Professional competence and skill are at stake.

In one church, thanks to a very generous discretionary fund placed completely under my control, I was able to finance continuing-education programs and invite many fellow ministers to attend. The church officials liked that and considered it an outreach of their ministry. Ministers' spouses also were invited to share in these experiences.

My experience in assisting other ministers to participate in programs of continuing education was so gratifying that I would strongly urge pastors to employ discretionary funds for that purpose. It has the possibility of making local churches aware of how they may contribute to ministerial education. It is one thing for local churches to expect that there will always be an available pool of pastors from which they might select their own; it is another for them to be concerned about pastors who are regularly enriched by programs of continuing education. These programs can be expensive, and the financial resources must come from somewhere. Indeed, the local church can come to enjoy this kind of fund as a significant part of its benevolence budget.

Lyle Schaller informs us that a growing number of congregations now identify themselves as "teaching churches," meaning that they provide continuing education for pastors other than those on their own staff. This is especially common among Presbyterian, Baptist (General Conference), Church of Christ, Evangelical Free, Disciples of Christ, Lutheran, and independent churches. Some United Church of Christ and Episcopal churches have done the same. In every case, the pastor of a teaching church would obviously be a key person in the administering of such programs. My experience meant so much to me that I count it as an important factor in what were for me the best years. It meant so much, in fact, that now in my retirement I have established my own foundation fund, so that this activity can be continued.

Continuing-education engagements, in whatever segments of a total career they may occur, definitely have a profound influence on what may be counted as best years. There is something exhilarating about subjecting one's mind and soul to new ideas and fresh insights, being stirred by new biblical concepts, having the windows of one's mind thrown open to the refreshing breezes of new scholarship and daring thoughts.

I have often pondered a brilliant line from the Academy Award-winning film *Chariots of Fire*. When Eric Liddell, the British missionary upon whose life the film was based, explained to his skeptical sister that he was preparing to run in the 1924 Olympics, he said that he believed God, in making him for a purpose, had created him with the ability to run very fast. "When I run," he told her, "I feel God's pleasure." Such clergy with that same sense of rightness, I daresay, would have many best years in the ministry.

Without renewal and refreshment, long pastorates could become a burden, or a mere matter of safe and selfish security. Feeling "comfortable" in a pastorate might really indicate stagnation. At age fifty-five, pastors might feel like settlers, with no inclination to move on, to accept the challenging changes of a new pastorate. With ten years or so to go, they might hope that the congregations would allow them to stay until retirement. If "comfort" is the controlling principle, pastors might think of these as the best years. But such "best years" may be at the cost of growing churches and vital ministry. In seeking comfort, not wanting to upset the carefully arranged applecart, the gospel may become muffled and vitality drained.

On the other hand, a long pastorate at age fifty-five can be challenging and energizing, if a pastor keeps growing and worries less about personal security. Indeed, some of the greatest pastorates have been very long, but they endured with vitality because the minister kept growing—intellectually, culturally, and spiritually.

When I was age fifty-seven, I was challenged to move from a church I dearly loved. There I had had some of the best years of my life. The church to which I went was faced with staggering problems, including a huge debt. I had to hit the parish "running," and I stayed there until I officially retired. And though I have loved every parish I have served, these last eight years were the best!

A pastor has many responsibilities, but the act of preaching probably sums them all up. When a preacher stands in a pulpit and feels a shivering, awesome sense of vocation, that preacher cannot really say that there ever have been any better years! It may very well be a serious warning to the preacher who feels a diminution of that awe at any time during a career. The pastor shares professional functions with those in other walks of life: administration, counseling, teaching, group leadership. But no other profession possesses the inherent command to preach.

A most telling observation, reported by Clark Morphew in the *St. Paul Pioneer Press Dispatch*, is drawn from a study by the American Lutheran Church, researched by Milo Brekke and Associates:

> People don't join churches because they like the members, are warmed by the greeters, or are beguiled by coffee-hour fellowshipers. To think that people do, says Morphew, is "baloney." . . . "For an hour on your first Sunday morning in

a church, your eyes and ears follow the hired help from podium to postlude, and if you are impressed, you're likely to make a return visit. If you're not impressed, if the sermon is boring, if there is no vision offered the worshipers, if the status quo is the only good news, you may not make much of an effort to darken the door of that church again."

(Context [May 1, 1987], p. 1)

Several years ago I was in a group that toured the magnificent St. Isaac's Cathedral in Leningrad. Our official Intourist guide, a very bright and scholarly young man, explained that in 1931, the government had transformed the cathedral into a museum. That explanation has pestered my mind every since. St. Isaac's is, indeed, a present-day museum of art. Throngs of people crowd it every day, marveling at its twenty-five Rembrandts, its priceless collection of French impressionists. Once it was filled with worshipers; now it is packed with tourists.

In transforming this cathedral into a museum, the most damaging blow the Soviet government inflicted, I believe, was that of enshrouding its pulpit in utter silence. The pulpit is still there as an object of artistic admiration, but it is empty and dead. I think this may be a potential parable for our churches. I would make this assertion: When a church, in the evangelical, biblical sense, allows its preaching to become perfunctory, dispirited, and bloodless, it is on the way to becoming a museum. If the preacher does not care, it *is* a museum.

It is not simple nostalgia to recall the impact of some of our great preachers of the past generation. Harry Emerson Fosdick was one. He preached to throngs of intellectuals on Morningside Heights in New York City, but it is striking to note how his biographer, Robert Moats Miller, ends a most stimulating chapter, "The Preparation and Presentation of Preachable Sermons":

> Fosdick's people wanted dignity and reason in the sermons of their minister and in that sense they were modernists; but

71

they were also heirs of nineteenth-century evangelism in that they did not want these qualities at the expense of a heartwarming experience. The ultimate court of appeal for every Christian remained: "Whereas once I was blind, now I see." The secret of Fosdick's appeal is that his sermon helped people to open their eyes and their hearts without insisting that they close their minds.

(Harry Emerson Fosdick: Preacher, Pastor, Prophet, pp. 377-78)

There may never be another Fosdick, but I am convinced that what our slumping churches need is a seismic jolt in the pulpit. Karl Barth's words in his essay "The Need of Christian Preaching" are certainly significant: "On Sunday morning when the bells ring to call the congregation and minister to church, there is in the air an *expectancy* that something great, crucial, and even momentous is to *happen*" *(The Word of God and the Word of Man,* p. 104). Barth goes on to say that this expectation rests in a special way on the preacher. The preacher is not the event, but only its voice.

One time when I was leading a group in a study of Letter to the Hebrews and explicating a difficult passage, I quoted an established scholar. A most perceptive member of the group then observed, "He must know something we don't know." Though that is a weighty responsibility, I have come to believe that that very thing is the role of the preacher-pastor—to know certain things that others do not know and to have the grace to articulate them.

Several years ago the distinguished columnist James Reston wrote, "President Reagan talks big but thinks small. He waves his bat like Babe Ruth and points to the right field bleachers, but then he bunts" *(Herald-Tribune* [overseas issue], June 17, 1985). Perhaps we preachers often are guilty of waving our bats and pointing presumptuously to great events, but in the pulpit we only bunt, because we are not wholeheartedly committed to preaching.

Stephen B. Oates, biographer of Martin Luther King, Jr., declares that his preaching "was the touchstone of his leadership" *(Let the Trumpet Sound,* p. 289). Leading and motivating the people of God in the church of Christ through preaching surely has much to do with the best years in the life of a pastor. If the modern malaise of our major denominations is to be arrested and reversed, the pastor as preacher will need to use those best years to sound the pulpit trumpets that never call retreat.

Indeed, many voices would loudly dispute this heavy emphasis on the importance of preaching. They would cite other issues that should be accorded equal ranking. Certainly no pastor can deny the importance of meaningful liturgy, music, Christian education, and pastoral diligence, and the best years for many pastors will be shaped and refined from gifts other than preaching prowess. But in the longer perspective, if there is not much depth and authenticity in the pulpit, the gratifications of ministry are likely to be depressed.

Preaching with some degree of effective power is not possible without a lifetime commitment to the disciplines of study. Certainly no one would say that the minister whose preaching gives the impression of "thumping the tub" is having good years. And an empty tub at that! It is a demanding task for a minister to preach a creditable sermon week after week, month after month, year after year. When a minister realizes that less and less time is being devoted to sermon preparation, that minister may very well determine that these may not be shaping up as the best years.

On the other hand, there is a deep sense of gratification and self-assurance when one enters the pulpit regularly on Sunday mornings, knowing that the sermon emerges out of toil and struggle. Indeed, the preacher's study might be thought of as a creative sweat shop. Those quickest to discern that the sermon comes from a crucible of struggle will be the listeners in the pews. Even though most sermons are flawed and finite, the knowledge of studious preparation constructs a sense of the best years.

A distinguished Presbyterian minister, Donald Morrison Meisel, tells me that on Tuesday of each week, he meets with his staff of five and shares with them the core idea of the sermon he is focusing on that week. Then he invites their input for its preparation, and they contribute helpful suggestions and enriching ideas, which he kneads into the sermon. Though he has been a minister for many years, he is obviously lengthening his best years by having the grace and maturity to invite his colleagues into the sermonic workshop.

During my best years—the last eight—I rented a room at a special retreat center, where I spent one full day a week. There I could concentrate in prayer, reflection, and study, and do serious research on the sermon idea bubbling formlessly in my mind. When I shut the door of that room, I had the assurance of knowing that the officials of the church I served approved wholeheartedly of this study retreat and did not consider it just a "day off."

Several qualities often distinguish the best years for many pastors. Consider the quality that grows from the relationships of depth, warmth, and responsiveness between pastor and people. As described in chapter 2, these are experiences of gratification fulfillment, especially when they are mutual. As the pastor moves among the people of the congregation, ministering to them in their joys and sorrows, their celebrations and their sufferings, the ties of their interaction bind them together in Christian love. This "fellowship of kindred minds" becomes "like that above." Then the pastor is grateful to be a minister. This is not to say there are no conflicts, irritations, differences, no troubled waters. It simply means that over all chasms, deep or shallow, pastor and people have built a bridge of caring and service.

Another quality of the best years is seen in the pastor's relationship with the community in which the church is located. No pastor can ignore a responsibility to the community at large. Many years ago a dear elderly woman encouraged me to believe that my service to the community was, in her view, an extension of my ministry. Profound personal rewards are to be gained by participating in community activities which provide services for all the people. These rewards are multiplied as the pastor joins with pastors of other denominations in vital programs and projects. The more a pastor learns to love the larger community of which the church is a part, the more good years will be experienced.

Still another quality of the best years comes from the realization that the people of the parish trust the pastor with their most personal problems and needs. In former times, ministers may not have been perceived as persons who could be entrusted with great burdens of guilt and wrongdoing. Indeed, there was a kind of phony relationship in which parishioners dreaded to learn that their pastor *knew* their inmost secrets and sins. Fortunately that has changed, and now pastors often are seen as caring persons who will not react judgmentally when such concerns as marital infidelity, divorce, homosexuality, or alcoholism are shared in the privacy of the pastor's study. If the pastor really cares, and persons of all backgrounds and experiences come for help and counseling, then an important ingredient of the best years has been added.

One more quality of the best years has to do with the pastor's own family. A minister's effectiveness and vitality are surely crippled when the spouse or children are unhappy and find no enjoyment in being part of a larger church family. But if those same family members find pleasure and meaning in the parish, their attitudes will escalate the compensations for the pastor.

Many years ago when I was a pastor in Columbus, Ohio, our family was thrilled to have as a guest at our dinner table one Sunday evening the fabulous Ohio State University track star Jesse Owens. He was to speak at a youth rally in our church that evening, and our children have never forgotten the incandescent presence of that man in our home. Because of that experience and others like it, our children loved that church, and when years later they learned that the old parsonage in which they grew up had burned, they wept. Their love for that church enhanced my love.

Recently I read three striking notes in the church newsletter of a ministerial friend of mine. Years ago in another city, I watched him go through a very difficult divorce and eventual separation from his children. In this newsletter, however, I noted that all his children, now grown, are actively participating in the church he is currently serving. That Sunday, two were listed as greeters and one—a young man—as attendant in the nursery. Their active presence in the church he serves certainly must be an encouragement to him. *These* may be his best years.

But for some, the best years of ministry can be seriously diminished by a number of potentially threatening episodes. Three of these need to be explored here.

First is the acknowledgment that the minister, like other human souls, can experience deep hurts. In the macho world of football and other contact sports, we hear a great deal about athletes playing while hurt. Occasionally some superb athletic performances are turned in by athletes who rise to heroic heights, though wincing with pain. And it is fair to say, I believe, that the pastor must often do the same.

Pastors can be easily hurt. Biting criticism can hurt, especially when it is perceived to be unjust. Prominent leaders who defect from the church cause deep pain. The rejection by officials of a carefully prepared plan for church programing can fill one with dismay. The decision not to grant a needed or expected salary increase is often interpreted as failure. Hurts occur over the refusal to make the minister's home a more decent habitation. Missing out on denominational promotion or recognition can plunge one into dark despair.

Though it may seem paradoxical, a pastor's best years can be realized in times of crisis. Wounded but not defeated, a pastor may rise to the occasion that creative leadership truly demands. The old aphorism, "A person should be like tea—the real strength appears in hot water," is especially true of the pastor. Though some may feel like overused tea bags, they must know how to deal creatively with conflict. Pastors hurt because parishioners hurt, and they often lash out against the person who is conveniently near. That person may very well be the pastor, who thus becomes a human punching bag.

There will be no best years for the pastor who cannot learn to love people despite their hostility, their pettiness, their prejudices, and their hang-ups. In the larger sense of parish issues, the best years will be determined by how the pastor responds to opposition. And opposition to the pastor, be it caused by life-style, ideas, or program proposals, is bound to occur. This sometimes requires a graciousness and magnanimity of spirit that few of us possess in our natural state, but unless we can rise to the occasion, we are sadly lacking in creative leadership. According to another football cliche, when the going gets tough, the tough get going. The pastor should make no boast about being "tough," but there must be a kind of toughness in the soul of the pastor who can endure without breaking and blanching.

One tough crisis a pastor may have to deal with often occurs when one's immediate predecessor happens to be very popular, leaving behind the "beloved pastor" ambience. Sometimes the new pastor discovers that the forerunner has carved out a pedestal of near-icon adoration. Often the incoming pastor will be troubled, perhaps tormented, by anthems of praise sung continually to the name of the pastor who has just left. The unending stanzas of affection can crash like cacophonies in the ears of the pastor who has been given the responsibility of continuing the ministry. But no ordination service ever promised a minister immunity from this kind of hurt, to say nothing of a rose garden.

The way the new pastor responds may very well determine whether these next years will be marked by misery and melancholy. This is the time, of course, to reveal the gifts of grace and guts. Instead of nursing this hurt, allowing it to fester and infect, the creative pastor responds with imagination and goodwill. Crying about it can only intensify the hurt. Rather, through grace and prayer, one might triumph by uttering every day the words from Psalm 103:1, 2:

> Bless the LORD, O my soul;
>   And all that is within me, bless his holy name!
> Bless the LORD, O my soul,
>   and forget not all his benefits.

Henri Nouwen, in the remarkable little book *The Wounded Healer*, describes the experience of every creative pastor:

> Since it is [the minister's] task to make visible the first vestiges of liberation for others, he must bind his own wounds carefully in anticipation of the moment when he will be needed. He is called to be the wounded healer, the one who must look after his own wounds but at the same time be prepared to heal the wounds of others. (p. 82)

The minister who understands and practices this faith is surely one whose best years will be indistinguishable from any other years.

Another threat to one's best years can be the green-eyed monster of covetousness. Often in the middle years of a career, pastors begin to feel that the profession is cheating them out of all the entitlements and pleasures that others in an affluent society seem to be enjoying. Many are no longer willing to accept the role of being as poor as Lazarus.

It is unsettling to some pastors to realize that though they are admired and respected by members of the congregation—indeed even esteemed as "men and women of God"—they are economic failures. They cannot participate fully in this quite materialistic age. If they live in the suburbs, they do not have all the "things" many of their parishioners have. Careful studies show that the incomes of ministers do not compare well with the incomes of other professionals, who often have fewer academic credits. This desire for some of the "good things" enjoyed by parishioners can become a deadly resentment in the minds of many pastors and quickly turn into an obsession.

A pastor suffering from this ailment is not likely to be moved by this paraphrase of a Commandment: "You shall not covet your neighbor's house, or his wife, or his manservant, or his maidservant, or his Mercedes, or his motor launch, or his snowmobile, or anything that is your neighbor's." Could it be that our resentment festers because we cannot decide whether the ministry is a profession, or a vocation—a "calling from God"?

The pastor may enjoy dinners set with elegant silver, the finest china, the choicest food, and glowing candlelight. There may be invitations to the country club and the downtown club and the many parties attended by the elite. But still there may persist a sense of alienation in the midst of splendor. On Sunday morning when the preacher looks out upon an assembly of yuppies, upward-bounds, the successful and prestigious, all glittering in the midst of just ordinary people, there may be the haunting fear that one does not really belong. Hence, despite much lavish entertainment and pampering, this kind of life may not add up to what many perceive to be the best years.

When we attempt to measure and assess our best years, we generally think in terms of a career. In discussing some of these career crises, a fellow minister, Larry Hilkemann, made a trenchant observation in declaring that there is a big difference between a *career* and a *calling*. It is worth contemplating. Traditionally ministers have been said to be "called." Our forebears in the ministry apparently did not perceive their calling to be in terms of privilege, entitlements, entertainment, even "success." Rather, they felt called to a life of service and commitment, even sacrifice. Thus, to fight off the demons of covetousness will require a new understanding of the ministry as a *calling*. Without this understanding, the best years are at stake.

There is still a third threat to the enjoyment of the best years. For many there is what might be called the loneliness of the long-distance pastor. As the years accumulate, some pastors, especially those whose ministry has built a reputation for effectiveness and respect, feel they are drifting into lonely isolation. Younger ministers tend to run in a kind of pack, exchanging social visits, playing golf and tennis, even vacationing as families together, certainly gossiping and speculating about local church and denominational politics. But as time and careers advance, there is often a discernible erosion of these relationships. Then loneliness.

Veteran pastors sometimes feel that younger ministers have excluded them from their more intimate cliques. Why they may do this is not clear, though it could be because of the image of "success" that surrounds older pastors, the prestigious pulpits they occupy, or just their age. It is possible, of course, that they may be perceived as aloof, infrequently attending the boiler-room denominational meetings where the nuts and bolts of church organization are measured and rearranged. Furthermore, they may not have bothered to participate in ministerial social and seasonal gatherings. Yet a growing sense of loneliness haunts what could otherwise be these pastors' best years.

Since many pastors belong to denominational families, those enjoying the best years because of a fund of mature experience might consider how they might offer encouragement and support to younger ministers who are struggling to find their way. Though operating from a heavy and demanding schedule, mature pastors might very well befriend younger ones, inviting them to lunch or entertaining a group in their home. In authentic acts of graciousness and generosity, the loneliness of the long-distance pastor may be mitigated.

One pastor in his middle years has said he finds it

necessary to keep the "right" company. He is not thinking of those with political clout, but of those who have positive and hopeful attitudes. "It is important to me," he says, "to be in the company of those who laugh a lot." This pastor feels it is not healthy to be in the presence of those who have soured on the ministry because they feel they have been cheated by circumstances. Furthermore, he does not want to remain too long in the company of those who have started the "winding down" process. Those pastors, he believes, are not likely to be uplifting and stimulating. To keep moving and alive for the best years, then, may be conditioned by the company one keeps.

If one does truly experience the loneliness of the long-distance pastor, there may, in truth, be the need to accept and learn to live with a large measure of loneliness. The best years of one's ministry may not be nurtured by running with a pack. Those who love the privilege of being ministers may need to take seriously what Dietrich Bonhoeffer said in *Life Together:* "Blessed is he who is alone in the strength of the fellowship and blessed is he who keeps the fellowship in the strength of aloneness" (p. 89).

The best years of ministry, then, will be realized in different ways and at different times by each individual. But the key to those years could be determined by those who have the grace to say, with the Apostle Paul: "For I have learned, in whatever state I am, to be content. I know how to be abased, and I know how to abound; in any and all circumstances I have learned the secret of facing plenty and hunger, abundance and want. I can do all things in him who strengthens me" (Phil. 4:11b-13 RSV). Learning that secret might enable one to experience the best years at many different times and places.

V

Pre-retirement

All pastors necessarily enter a pre-retirement stage, when thought and planning must be devoted to what lies ahead. Some have referred to this stage as "winding down." The baseball season winds down during the World Series, the hunting season winds down to the last two legal days, and the administration of a United States President winds down toward exit from the White House. And yet the term for a pastor has troubling ambiguities. The analogy of "winding" suggests a clock or some other coiling mechanism. Is the pastor preparing to go on some kind of "slow" time? Will he or she begin to sound like an old phonograph record, trailing off in a whine? Is the pastor becoming unwound?

Frankly, I have problems with the concept of "winding down." I would like to believe that pastors can plan the various career stages so that it is possible to arrive at the official date of retirement with an attitude and enthusiasm for ministry that enable them to leave with joy-filled hearts. If a pastor is viewed as manifestly winding down, it seems likely that the members of the church will be cheated by a less than full-throttle effort. Furthermore, such a pastor may be less than an inspiration and example to younger pastors. In the previous chapter I cited a minister who said that he does not care to linger in the company of those who have started the winding-down process.

One lay person reported that after the minister of the church had announced the date of his retirement, a pronounced change was evident in his ministry. "He went limp on us," was the charge. Perhaps that minister saw in his retirement date a reason to pull up or slow down, but to "go limp" is to give a message about how one views the ministry. Are not the people of a congregation entitled to a full-service ministry, whether the minister be young, middle-aged, or about to retire? Going limp might call forth some of the euphemistic put-downs regarding below-par behavior. Could it be said of some pastors at this stage: Her elevator doesn't go all the way to the top any more? He's operating one quart low? He's rowing with only one oar? Pastors with pride and self-respect certainly will want to guard against giving the impression that they have taken the foot off the accelerator and are simply coasting downhill.

One minister told me that a big change was observed in his predecessor after the third addition was built onto the church. Then he just coasted toward retirement, losing all interest in further innovations, his ignition shut off. It was as though he felt he had fulfilled his ministry, and the congregation should indulge his idleness until it was time to give him a retirement party. He seemed to be saying to the people that he had run out of gas and did not want to be towed in for refueling. He had taken down his sails and had no intention of raising them again to find new and fresher winds. Indeed, to watch someone slide into sloth is a sorry sight—and a hurtful reflection on the Christian ministry.

In these pre-retirement years, pastors tend to drift into mediocrity if no goals are set. With one eye fixed on the retirement date, it is a temptation to regard goal-setting as irrelevant, requiring no sense of urgency. If these crucial years are not to be dissipated in disinterest, personal goals become imperative. It might, for example, become easy for a pastor to lose all interest in recruiting new members. One pastor in his early sixties recently complained that he was sick and tired of being burdened with the call for church growth. During the whole of his ministry, this necessity had been laid upon him, and now he is weary of such commands.

But this is the precise moment when pastors, lest they go limp, should set goals consciously and deliberately. In my last pastorate, I determined that our downtown church should be receiving at least one hundred new members each year. That difficult task became a sacred goal, and each year we came close or actually reached that goal.

Though most pastors in their pre-retirement years would be reluctant to have such goals set for them, these years might be energized if each church, as a corporate body, set those goals. Actually, a church would be well advised, by setting goals which the pastor would be expected to strive for, to protect itself from a pastor who simply pines away. It is unjust for a parish to disintegrate because its pastor is unraveling toward retirement.

The zeal with which a pastor finishes the ministry says much about commitment and preparedness at the beginning. Every minister, at some time, has preached a sermon that echoed the famous words of the Apostle Paul: "The time of my departure has come. I have fought the good fight, I have finished the race, I have kept the faith" (II Tim. 4:6b-7 RSV). But can anyone imagine Paul going limp during the last two or three years of his mission?

That passage seems to be drawn from a set of metaphors from the athletic arena. "Fight" seems to apply to a wrestling match; "race" obviously suggests a long distance run; "faith" surely has to do with the athlete's pledge to keep the rules. Unlike the experience of most pastors, "departure" must refer to Paul's impending martyr's death.

But when people commit to the ministry, if they are realistic, they will expect to engage in lifelong wrestling matches with all kinds of adversaries, including administrative boards, trustees, finance committees. Do they not realize at the beginning that a ministerial career means a long-distance race? And what about the pledge of faithfulness one makes at the starting line—the ordination vows? Is there any justification for dropping out of the race or slowing down before the finish line is reached?

Individual pastors may have different reasons for the style and manner in which they manage the last few months or years of their pastorates. Some reasons may truly legitimatize a change of pace or a slowing down of action and energy levels. But even with allowances for health or disability, one does not need to drift into a near-comatose state. It is not a mere macho performance for someone to die in harness, like a horse that drops dead between two shafts of a cart. We seem to admire people who die with their boots on. In the case of pastors, could we not say we respect those who arrive at the day of retirement with their running shoes on?

Of course, several possible scenarios could be written for the pre-retirement process. One is almost mandated when a pastor becomes physically or emotionally disabled. I know of a church that suffered through five years of its pastor's inability to function. In addition to a physical ailment, he had become addicted to alcohol, making for a most difficult situation. At issue were not only the pastor's health, but his financial and economic security as well. It is extremely painful for a sensitive congregation to deal with this kind of situation. Most denominations do not have sufficient funds to cushion any arrangements that could settle the crisis, yet such a pastor is being actually "wound down" by the cruel twists of fate and circumstance.

One thing seems clear: A local church caught in this kind of crisis cannot be expected to endure the erosion of pastoral leadership indefinitely. If there is multiple staff, other staff members can bridge the leadership gap for a time, but that time must be kept within reasonable limits. No emergency solutions being available, the only possible resolution would seem to require a combination of congregational generosity (in terms of special funds), denominational contingency funds, the support of the pastor's family, insurance, and the provisions of Social Security. To say the least, this kind of winding down uncoils into a tangled set of hardships for everyone concerned.

Another possible scenario is sometimes written for the middle-aged pastor who may be five or ten years from retirement but would like to reduce the heavy pressure which falls upon the senior pastor. Such a pastor could seek a call or appointment as an associate pastor. Chapter three suggests the associate as an option at the beginning of one's career; here I mention it as a late choice. This venture has its waiting beds of quicksand, but for some it has been an acceptable alternative to the bearing of an onerous responsibility. It does not necessarily mean that the pastor's energy level decelerates, but that he or she is simply willing to step out of the captain's seat and become a member of the crew. This kind of shift happens all the time in the academic field when scholars no longer feel they can shoulder the burden of chairing departments. It can be a way of winding down without copping out.

It may be said that such pastors are freed to devote their gifts to what they do best. It could be pastoral calling, or financial management, or even direction of the church school. It may be, frankly, a way of avoiding the buck-stops-here syndrome, letting another senior pastor deal with the problems. Reducing the anxiety and tension borne by the pastor-in-charge, therefore, may be a creative way to continue in vital ministry while winding down with integrity.

In still another scenario, pastors in their later years might take a denominational position that would afford release from the heavy day-to-day pressures of a pastorate. This could provide a change of venue in which a pastor would be thrust, ironically, into multiple venues. Often a denominational post requires much traveling and one-night stands, meeting with congregations in different locations. Indeed, the term *venue* still suggests the necessity of appearing before a jury that will judge one's competence and effectiveness. Yet no such jury would subject a minister to the almost total scrutiny and cross-examination that occurs in a parish. As the years advance, some pastors no longer feel emotionally and physically able to take the heat. Not ready to retire, a pastor may discover this mode a reasonable and respectable alternative.

One pastor carefully considered such a move when asked to submit to a denominational board job interview. Fifty-five years of age and having just suffered a disturbing physical illness, he reasoned that this might be a viable alterative to his present situation. Furthermore, the church he was presently serving was faced with the huge task of a new building development and unprecedented growth. He was not sure he was up to it. The new position would also give him the opportunity to acquire a home suitable for retirement. Pondering these possibilities in no way marred this pastor's integrity. His very self-evaluation indicated his concern for the welfare of the congregation and the period of expansion it was entering. He was concerned lest his own personal limitations be inadequate to lead that development. Eventually, for many good reasons, he decided not to seek the functionary role and remained with the congregation, recommitting his considerable talents to their mission. But for other pastors weighing a similar move, taking a denominational position might be the better part of wisdom and Christian stewardship.

Still other alternatives exist for pastors in the middle years. One is the possibility of serving as an interim minister. Many churches searching for a new permanent pastor would be well served with an interim person, especially when the minister who just left was popular and effective. A cushion of time and transition often makes it easier for a succeeding minister to assume the responsibility later. When the loss of a beloved pastor causes grief, even anger, a time for healing and recovery is in order, and the interim pastor serves this purpose very well. Such service can become a vital stimulus and challenge to pastors who can call upon their experience without the apprehension of being rejected for a permanent term.

Indeed, in interim pastorship there is a healthy kind of freedom—freedom from the ambition to succeed to the position permanently. Thus the interim person is better able to assess the true needs of the congregation. If the members are grieving over the loss of a cherished pastor, the interim can listen to their feelings and help them accept what cannot be changed. If they have just expelled a pastor they found unacceptable, the interim can play a key role in helping evaluate the factors that caused a failed relationship. Insights and new attitudes might emerge which could contribute substantially to building a better relationship with the next permanent pastor. In all this, the intentional interim pastor may discover a most creative way to wind down.

In addition to these options, there is always the opportunity—in some denominations—for the experienced pastor to become bivocational. Perhaps there has always been the desire to venture into another field such as teaching, counseling, or administration. One would not necessarily need to leave the ministry entirely, but could become a part-time staff member or a weekend pastor in a smaller church. A pastor could move toward retirement while enjoying the good aspects of two worlds.

It might very well seem equally prudent to decide that one's career could be enriched by deliberately seeking the challenge of one more pastorate. But with the finish line of retirement in view, this would be difficult for many to do. Leaving the safety and security of a satisfactory pastorate just to seek one more brand-new parish might seem too risky and demanding. Yet such a final venture might be a way to prevent one from going limp.

Limpness could also be avoided in some cases by seeking a parish in another state or denomination. Such opportunities may be severely limited, but they are not impossible. I heard of one minister who had spent fourteen years in a prestigious church. Feeling that his ministry might be going stale and finding no other place available, he was successful in transferring to another denomination. This made it possible to accept a call to a parish in another state, which projected him into a quite different but challenging environment. His last years find him with a new lease on life and on the ministry.

Though at the outset I suggested that the pre-retirement process is loaded with a number of ambiguities, I think it needs to be candidly acknowledged that most pastors must deal with its reality in some measure. Our humanity would seem to dictate the confession that most of us, even in our youth, fantasize about what we might do when the ringing of the church bell no longer stirs in us a Pavlovian response to pastoral duties. These conditioned reflexes are admittedly hard to break, but we seem to have a secret yearning for the more leisurely life. The trouble is that this yearning, even unconsciously, can narcotize our zeal.

Lest we wind down to lower levels of faithfulness, we can cope with the perils of what might be called ministerial menopause in several ways. Continuing education and the search for fresher ways to do ministry have already been mentioned.

When I was a young pastor, I had one of the most electrifying experiences of my life: the privilege of being a member of the late Sherwood Eddy's famous 1950 American Seminar—an eight-week study tour of Europe, in which Dr. Eddy introduced us to some of the great personalities and scholars. We listened to such people as Arnold Toynbee, the poet Stephen Spender, Lady Astor, and the famous Red Dean of Canterbury. We saw the ruins of London and Berlin. I came home with my mind chock-full of history and insights into the nature of humanity.

But I knew that however rich and powerful that one

experience had been, it would need to be repeated and renewed. In subsequent years, therefore, I sought the excitement of being further exposed to great minds and great experiences. I found this in Union Seminary's summer Conferences for Ministers in New York City and at the Princeton Institute of Theology. Others have found similar enrichment at Kirkridge, the Alban Institute, and countless travel-study seminars abroad. Let me boldly submit a rule of conduct for every pastor entering the pre-retirement stage: Thou must, every year, enroll in a respectable and demanding program of continuing education. If you do this sincerely and expectantly, very few will accuse you of going limp.

As one grows older and begins to plan for retirement, there is a tendency to avoid certain kinds of activities and responsibilities. Two of those activities are working with youth and making pastoral calls. Though not all pastors at the age of fifty-five can serve as Pied Pipers, many can be most effective. Hence one does not need to give up this responsibility entirely. Confirmation classes are excellent means of affording pastors the opportunity to keep a finger on the pulse of youth. It is a precious privilege to relate to young people in this way. Then on that day of confirmation when the pastor lays hands on their heads in the sacrament of grace, they are not strangers or mere numbers, but rather the beloved children of the parish who have touched the pastor's heart most intimately. On the day of confirmation, the pastor is not so much winding down as winding up!

The pastor also can sustain effectiveness in the closing years of a career by making a deliberate effort to call in the homes of parishioners and prospective members. As one grows older, it is tempting to let someone else do the calling, even rationalizing that lay people need to do it in order to be witnessing Christians. It is also tempting to stay home in one's easy chair, flipping TV channels with the remote control. But to keep alive and retire with honor, a pastor needs to know the people of the parish by visiting in their homes, sharing their thoughts and feelings. Depending on the size of the church, the pastor may not need to do all the necessary calling alone, but ministry is more viable when the pastor takes a share.

Chapter three speaks of making an average of four hundred weekly personal contacts with parishioners. This suggests that the pastor who is contemplating the end of a career needs to have some plan for one-on-one contacts, whether they be in individual homes or through the church's programmatic life. At no stage of a pastorate is there an excuse for avoiding or eliminating pastoral contact.

Having faced honestly some of the perils and temptations of the closing years of active ministry, it must be clearly asserted that pastors dare not come to the final day without having given some attention to what they will be doing the day after the party. It is prudent to make some plans. Some pastors have arrived at the time when they will assume almost total self-responsibility without any idea what they are going to do or where they will live.

I have a remarkable friend whose only plan prior to retirement was to live in a travel trailer. In twelve years, he has traveled literally all over the world, constantly on the move. A widower, he apparently did not have the usual need for a permanent dwelling. He has had an exuberant time doing exactly as he chooses, though his plan is quite exceptional.

Some ministers who come to their final day without having made any provision for a dwelling probably never have had the financial means to purchase a home. They have managed by renting and possibly by living with relatives. Since in the last decade or two there has been a proliferation of church-sponsored retirement homes, it is often quite satisfactory to seek this kind of housing. Other ministers have invested in income property with a double benefit. The purchase of a duplex provides not only a place to live but additional income. Obviously, such an arrangement requires planning in the closing years.

Perhaps the professional ministry should have a kind of counterpart to professional football's two-minute warning. This presumably gives the coach and team an opportunity to plan and possibly change their strategy during the last two minutes of the game. Being forced into such final decision making in the required time-out may result in winning the game. How long the two-minute period would translate realistically into a pastor's situation cannot be exactly measured. It might be two years, or one year, or six months, but it would seem mandatory that some such warning signal be employed.

The Presbyterian Church (USA) does give a two-minute warning (actually a ten-year warning). The Board of Pensions writes each minister who turns fifty-five, encouraging the development of retirement strategies if such plans have not been made. Pre-retirement seminars are offered around the country for all clergy, but especially for those age forty and over.

Setting a specific date for retirement, and announcing it, might very well be a vital catalyst. In some denominations the pension board will allow only a certain time frame in which to set the retirement date. Still, there is a sense of freedom for pastors who can study all the options and necessities, then make the decision themselves. It then becomes a definite factor in the pre-retirement process—one that can conceivably affect the quality of ministry in whatever time remains. There is no reason to keep this decision a secret. The parish pulpit committee has a right to know; the people of the parish have a right to know. Then pastors are free—wonderfully free—to offer themselves wholeheartedly to vibrant ministry during the remaining days.

What is the best time for this decision? Some denominations mandate the retirement age at 70 or 68 years. Some have not mandated any age, but 65 has become prevalent, this being the age at which Social Security income can be fully realized. The amount of Social Security income is considerably more at age 65 than at 62 or 59. Perhaps the Social Security Administration has inadvertently encouraged people to decide upon retirement at 65, and this has become a kind of unofficial, mind's-eye milestone that facilitates decision.

Since this is a very individual, almost existential decision, let me share the procedure that led to my retirement at age sixty-five. As I have stated, I loved the church I was serving on my sixty-fourth birthday. My perception was that the church was alive and well. Though I could hear at least a few faint knocks and snarlings, I believed that my ministry was generally well received. Many exciting things were happening. Though ours was a downtown church, our membership was showing annual gains.

The community, boasting a great university and the state capital, was a most stimulating and challenging place to be. I was gratified to have several roles of leadership in the community at large, and my wife and I enjoyed many of the rich cultural benefits of the city. I loved the people of the parish and, during eight years, had shared deeply and intimately through births, weddings, surgeries, deaths, serious illnesses, and countless family crises. And most highly prized was the sense that they accorded me freedom of the pulpit.

With only a few physical aches and pains, I was grateful for abundant health. Then after carefully weighing and assessing all these factors, I came to a sudden realization and decision: Now was the time to go! Indeed, I felt I could have continued for five more years, until The United Methodist Church told me it was time to retire. But I found myself singing (lustily, as John Wesley directed!):

> Through many dangers, toils, and snares,
> I have already come;
> 'Tis grace hath brought me safe thus far,
> And grace will lead me home.

And why, I asked, expect more of grace and push the graciousness of my congregation further? Why not leave now, while many of the parish could say, "Pastor, we are sorry to see you go," rather than three years later, hear them possibly say, "Pastor, we are sorry, but you must go!"?

It is not easy for anyone, let alone a pastor, to assess honestly and fearlessly one's own gifts and graces in the pre-retirement years. A huge ego is at stake, restless and insistent upon its claims. Here again, professional ministers may not be much different from professional athletes. We have watched baseball stars, boxing luminaries, football idols struggling to prove that Father Time has not touched them. But sometimes it is pitiful to watch the aging pitcher whose once blazing fast ball has cooled into mediocrity; the ancient fighter who is punched into a stumbling stupor; the gridiron great who has lost a step—all thinking they could do it one more time. Pastors growing older are no different. They too need the courage to face reality, so that they can retire from full professional life without being pitied.

Once the retirement date has been determined and announced, the pastor must face up to two other major responsibilities: Decide where to live during retirement, and make careful preparations for the coming of a successor.

The choice of a location for retirement is of crucial importance. One can always use common sense, but the absence of strict guidelines and principles often spells trouble. Denominational wisdom seems generally lacking, so let it be forthrightly asserted: When a retiring minister decides to remain in the community last served, harassment and discomfort are frequently created for the pastor who follows.

Of course, the retiring pastor never intends it to turn out that way. For many, the last parish served seems to be the most natural and felicitous environment. The pastor knows the community, feels comfortable there, and may very well own a home. Besides, it is an effort to make one last move into a new community where one will need to put down new roots. Furthermore, the pastor may enjoy the acceptance and place that have been achieved locally. The retiree may sincerely disavow any intention of interfering with the new minister. Besides, many have retired in the community last served and, on the surface, all appears to be well.

The problem is that what appears on the surface is often deceiving. When asked whether the predecessor should remain in the community, the incoming pastor is placed in a position of near intimidation. To object to this arrangement would certainly appear ungracious and petty, perhaps indicating a posture of insecurity, especially if the retiree had earned the accolade of "beloved pastor." Indeed, members of the congregation may make it plain that they want the former minister to stay in the community in a kind of unofficial emeritus role.

It cannot be denied that some satisfactory emeritus relationships have existed for outstanding pastors who have served landmark churches. A prominent example occurred when Harry Emerson Fosdick retired from Riverside Church in New York City in 1946. It is true that Fosdick's successor, Dr. Robert J. McCracken, insisted that Fosdick remain as minister emeritus and that Fosdick, with deep reluctance, accepted. Fosdick stayed in the church in a greatly reduced role, occasionally preaching, sometimes reading Scripture or offering the pastoral prayer. In his excellent biography previously referred to, Robert Moats Miller states:

> It must be emphatically insisted that Fosdick did not press his continuing service; his hand did not need to be pried from the tiller. Indeed, in 1947, after only one year, he absolutely refused to continue to receive an honorarium. . . . Even more significant, in January 1947 he firmly ordered that his name as minister emeritus be no longer printed in the church publications at the top of the list of ministers, expressing regret that he had ever allowed himself to be persuaded to the listing in the first place. (pp. 551-52)

Though this may have been an exception that proves the rule, in the overwhelming number of cases, this covenant does not work. Without pretending in any way to have special insight as to the cause, it must be noted that Robert J. McCracken did suffer a nervous breakdown during his first Christmas season at Riverside Church. The biographer offers no diagnosis and reports only that Fosdick's continuing presence was a steadying, healing factor. But let a general rule be stated clearly: In the pre-retirement years, the minister should consider all possibilities for settlement and then heed this command—Get out!

Repeatedly, the soundness of this rule has been proved. I have suffered vicariously as I watched clergy struggle with the imperious presence of predecessors whose intentions may have been of the best, but who, being within easy reach by phone, become parties to every parish dispute and disaffection. To be sure, a retiree may be reached by long-distance, but if complainers must pay for a call, it is less likely that they will register grievances.

I know of one retiree whose encampment in the parish, teaching Sunday school, taking on weddings and funerals, and serving on committees, caused his successor so much anguish that in what should have been his best years, he was struck with a psychic injury so deep that he never fully recovered.

Therefore, let us conclude that one of the most important and virtuous decisions made in this pre-retirement period is to seek a location elsewhere. This last decision could forever characterize one's ministry as just and caring. We might paraphrase the all-too-facile slogan, America—Love It or Leave It, by suggesting that if you truly love a parish, you will leave it when your time is up!

The other major responsibility in the pre-retirement process is the effort made to prepare the way for a successor. Here the influence of the outgoing minister can become profound and pervasive. No one else in the parish has such a key role. If ever "Amazing Grace" is needed, it is here. In this role the pastor who is winding down a career can effectively wind up the possibilities for the one who will assume the mantle of ministerial leadership.

If one spends the last months or last year doing all that can be done to fine-tune the church body as though it were a musical instrument, the incoming pastor will be greeted by mellifluous sounds of hope and encouragement. Possibly the most helpful thing an outgoing pastor can do is to build in the congregation the expectation that the new pastor will bring fresh gifts, graces, and ideas that will open doors to new visions of Christian witness. Here the function is to teach the congregation that no pastor is all-knowing and all-skilled, that new leadership should be welcomed and encouraged.

Of course, it is important that a realistic picture be drawn of the church's weaknesses and strengths, failures and achievements. But there is really no excuse for leaving the church in shambles, a state of disrepair. One pastor told me that when he went to be interviewed by a church from which the minister was retiring, he was so appalled by the shabby condition of the sanctuary that he almost aborted the meeting. The walls were grimy, the paint peeling. The spirit of the church, too, was in disarray. Such is the heritage that some retirees leave behind.

Is it possible that some pastors come down to the end of their career content to let the paint peel and the congregation fill with despair? One wonders if a pastor who leaves a church in such a derelict state was ever really wound up in the first place. The pre-retirement period may in one sense affirm the immortal words of Robert Browning:

> Grow old along with me!
> The best is yet to be,
> The last of life, for which the first was made:
> Our times are in his hand.
> > "Rabbi Ben Ezra"

Browning was evoking images of old age and eternity, but here also we find a suggestion of the way a pastor may experience the last year, months, or weeks of a career. Assuredly, when one is older, it is possible to experience the best years, the best times, very near the end. If our calling is truly in God's hand, this *can* be "the last of life, for which the first was made." It is possible to leave the profession with pulses pounding, sails unfurled—not trudging, but walking lightly. And sometimes, one of the severest tests of ministry can be sprung near the end.

That is what happened to me. As the day of the retirement party approached, my wife and I were enjoying farewell dinners and sentimental gatherings. Then on Friday morning, just two weeks before my last Sunday, I received an alarming message. The wife of our minister of music called to say that her husband, one of my dearest friends, was missing. He had not appeared for choir rehearsal the night before, and he had not come home. She had not seen him since early the day before, when he waved as he drove away from home. A distinguished professor, and the chair of the university's School of Music for sixteen years, he had apparently gone to his office to post the grades for the term just ending.

The day was radiant with spring, but an ominous cloud of fear and apprehension moved across our horizon. With the most troubled heart I had known during my years in the ministry, I drove to the family home. For the next twenty-four hours, I was with the family and in close touch with the campus police chief, whose force was searching everywhere.

One of the first things I noticed when I arrived at their home was a large package of brochures. They were the programs my friend and his wife had prepared for our farewell reception, scheduled for the coming Sunday. On the cover was our picture. Two years before, I had organized a gala banquet to celebrate his twenty years of brilliant leadership in our church and community. Now he and his wife were the organizers of this farewell for us.

As the day wore on, our church family and the university family were chilled in anxious waiting. A mystery of immense magnitude was enveloping us. Saturday morning came, and the police called me to report that the car had been found amid the ruined buildings of an abandoned farm not far away. I was alerted for another call, which came all too quickly, that the lifeless body had been found about sixty feet from the car. He had caused his own death by stabbing himself with a knife. I turned from the phone to inform and comfort his wife and children.

Questions of towering mystery and bewilderment loomed over our heads. Within less than twenty-four hours, it would be Sunday morning, time for our community of faith to gather for worship. On Saturday evening I went with the family to the funeral home. Later that night, I sat in my study at the church, searching for a way to minister meaningfully to the people I loved so dearly, knowing they had been plunged into the deepest grief, tormented by questions unanswered and unanswerable. I ransacked the depths of my being to serve them as pastor.

Sunday came, and the congregation gathered as a grieving family. I sought to remind the people I loved so much that despite our knowledge and caring, no one can know all the inner dramas being enacted in another human soul. Sometimes those who exude strength and confidence may be suffering unspoken hurt. The utterly gracious person may be suffering from rejection and indifference. I recalled for the congregation a vivid memory of my dear friend sitting at a football game alone, the rain pouring down upon his head. I reminded them that every human soul is a microcosm of nature, and sometimes, with devastating suddenness, a tornado may strike. As a church family, we gathered in our sorrow for comfort, strength, hope, and faith. I assured them that God would not allow us to hurt more than we could bear. We would survive.

On Monday evening a memorial service was held in our sanctuary, which seats only six hundred people. But from every quarter of the city and from around the state came twelve hundred people, overflowing into every hall and available room. And again my very soul was wrenched as I sought to be a pastor in this, the most critical event in my ministry.

On the following Sunday my wife and I said farewell and drove out of the city. I was retired. All that had happened in the last two weeks. It was a stage of my life as a pastor to which I could never return.

Winding down? Not as long as one has life and breath, as long as one is called to be a pastor of the people of God, as long as life surprises and stuns, as long as people are hurt and angry, as long as they are numbed by mystery and doubts, as long as they experience joy, hope, faith, and love. Let the pastor ponder always these matchless words of Robert Frost, from "Stopping by Woods on a Snowy Evening."

> The woods are lovely, dark and deep,
> But I have promises to keep,
> And miles to go before I sleep,
> And miles to go before I sleep.

VI

Postlogue:
Early Retirement Vocation

On the day after retirement, the pastor does not need to take up residence in the pits. For some, of course, retirement from the ministry means immersion in misery. Once again I cite one of my favorite cartoon strips, "The Small Society." Several years ago a disconsolate man was pictured sitting alone on a park bench. He was saying to himself, "Hoo-boy! Retirement should be the reward for a lifetime of work— instead, it's become a sort of punishment for growing old." Some retired pastors may feel they are being punished for growing old. But it doesn't need to be that way!

Behold the recycled minister! If old tires, newspapers, aluminum cans, and oil can be recycled, so can ministers. In the five years since my official retirement I have been recycled twice. When I retired, I did not feel that I was through. Thanks to an invitation from Eugene Winkler, one of my former students at St. Paul School of Theology, my ministry continued. Dr. Winkler, pastor of the Community United Methodist Church in Naperville, Illinois, invited me to join his church staff in a part-time role. He bestowed upon me the generous and extravagant title of Parish Minister, and soon I was calling upon hundreds of prospective members in a burgeoning suburban area. In addition, he invited me to organize a program I had instituted at two other churches, Books-Between-Bites, a noontime book-review program. Far from feeling punished, I felt exhilarated, almost "born again."

After three years in Naperville, I was recycled a second time. Seymour Halford invited me to join his church staff in Batavia, Illinois, where I actually live, as Minister of Program. Following a concept recommended by Lyle E. Schaller, I was given the opportunity to develop new programs for the church, and once again, Books-Between-Bites became a hit idea. Then my portfolio was extended to include calling on prospective members in that expanding community. No punishment here, either.

A retired minister is not necessarily worn out. Long ago, happily, The United Methodist Church discarded the term *worn out preacher*, which once described members of the clergy who had been retired. No doubt in the hardship days of the frontier, many preachers were withdrawn from service because they were simply "worn out." But I know some young, highly educated pastors who are worn out after the first year.

The Methodist tradition then chose another word to describe the condition of their aging clergy: *superannuated.* This term was in vogue when I began my ministry, but I didn't bother to look up its meaning until later. Then it became a cuss word. It means "retired because of age or infirmity . . . too old for use, work, or service . . . antiquated or obsolete." Those are fighting words, and I won't accept them. I don't need to take that kind of characterization!

If you are not worn out, you can be worthily and usefully recycled. Retired ministers are being effectively employed, usually part-time, on the staffs of parishes. Since many ministers now retire at age sixty-five or younger, they constitute a panel of pastoral experience available to local churches, generally on a half-time basis. Lyle Schaller thinks there are fewer retired ministers entering this kind of service now than there were ten or fifteen years ago. As reasons for this, he cites improved pension systems, employed spouses with their own pensions, and rising secular employment. Salary arrangements for retired ministers are often limited by Social Security restrictions. In 1989, a retired person sixty-five years of age or older on Social Security could earn no more than $8,800; a person under age sixty-five could earn no more than $6,480. After reaching the age of seventy, a person is no longer limited in the amount earned.

For all practical purposes, the retired pastor might be expected to work approximately twenty hours a week. As a full-time active pastor, I had no concept of punching a time clock, and I still am reluctant to keep track of the hours I devote each week to my recyclement. In some cases, it might very well be necessary for the church to require the recycled pastor to give an exact accounting of time spent. "Goofing off" can scarcely be tolerated! But in the two post-retirement positions I have held, my employers seemed to trust me to be conscientious about my stewardship of hours.

Generally speaking, an important feature in the economics of recycled pastors is the provision that they will secure their own housing, without a housing allowance. It is assumed that they will have planned and prepared for their retirement home. The proximity of that housing, of course, is important. Working in Naperville was not difficult because my home was only twelve miles away. Of course, when I joined the staff in Batavia, my driving time was greatly reduced.

Lyle Schaller, whose far-ranging experience as church consultant makes him privy to many post-retirement arrangements, suggests that the retiree may obtain double recycling in any given year. One might join a church staff in the Sunbelt for five months of the year; then, after a month's vacation, find employment on the staff of a church in the Frostbelt during summer and early fall. This would offer an exceptional advantage to each of those churches, in that the peripatetic pastor would be available in precisely those periods of the church year when most needed. And such a pastor would have the personal advantage of enjoying at least two months' vacation.

In addition, retired ministers could make themselves available for intentional interim assignments. With equal felicity, they might be most meaningfully recycled in small churches that never have had a full-time resident. In this way, pastors would enjoy comparative freedom from the burden of a full-time parish where the expectations of a work schedule are very high, while at the same time contributing the rich benefits and wisdom of mature experience.

Any one of these relationships could actually be a bargain for many smaller, medium-sized, or larger churches. The financial arrangements may be quite within their reach. Of course, recycled pastors better not have too many hang-ups about being a "bargain." Presumably they are beyond the stage of being neurotically anxious about salary scales. If a church is excessively stingy or exploitive, pastors are free to choose not to serve.

Being recycled has been a most attractive option for me, because I personally gained immense benefits from six different recycled ministers who served on my church staffs. It must, of course, be acknowledged that such benefits are not automatically guaranteed. Not every minister is a promising prospect for recycling. Some simply are not suited for this kind of relationship. But those with whom I have worked, one of whom was a retired bishop, both enriched and rewarded me.

Because this kind of recycling carries such potential benefits for both the church and the retired ministers, I would like to suggest the following cautions and observations:

1. Ministers being thus recycled might well think of themselves as similar to a kind of retread. Like a retreaded tire, the casing may be still strong and usable, but the tread will be in a different pattern. Compared to being a pastor-in-charge, as each may once have been, retired pastors still at work must learn to tread lightly. The in-charge

role is no longer for them. Now free from the major responsibilities involved in directing a parish, recycled pastors must guard against looseness of the lip. They were not installed as everflowing fountains of wisdom and superior knowledge. There is no call for the daily offering of this-is-the-way-I-did-it. If a staff member or the directing minister should invite suggestions, experience may be appropriately shared. Otherwise, the art of stifling the habit of reminiscence must be cultivated.

2. It ought to be a cardinal rule that unless a retiree can respect and honor the senior pastor, the position ought to be declined. The recycled pastor's authenticity in this role will be determined by the way the retiree perceives the authenticity of the head pastor. If the retiree cannot conscientiously support the directing pastor, then it is the wrong job. Undermining and sowing subtle seeds of contempt for the head pastor must be considered unconscionable. In one sense, this position is bestowed by the grace of the lead pastor, and the recycled pastor needs to accept graciously the privilege of still having a ministry. If there is a feeling of exploitation, of dignity and integrity abused, the most sensible recourse is to quit.

The relational chemistry is very important. When Bishop Ralph T. Alton became my colleague as Bishop-in-Residence, some of my fellow ministers thought, frankly, that I was foolhardy. "A bishop on your staff?" they groaned, ever so vicariously. "Why, he will continue to do just what a bishop always does—push you all over the parish."

But I knew that bishop, and I had no fear of being strong-armed by his episcopal muscle. He did, in fact, become my own pastor. Since the senior pastor often has a somewhat lonely role, I frequently found myself turning to the bishop to share my problems and hopes, always benefiting from his knowledge and experience. At the same time, he always was aware that I was the pastor-in-charge. To

105

be sure, some bishops might eviscerate you, but not that one. I never felt threatened.

Such a pattern may not be translatable into every situation. The senior pastor may be so extremely talented and secure that no effort is made to consult others about even major decisions. In that case the retired pastor must learn to keep a prudent distance—and closed mouth. On the other hand, the senior pastor may express a different personality, and a warm and rewarding relationship of trust and mutual sharing may develop. The recycled pastor may be perceived as a mentor, not a hired hand.

But never, never should the retiree, even unconsciously, seek to commandeer the decision-making dynamics of the church. If the recycled person has visions of parish-plums, let the trumpet call retreat! After all, that one may have had more than forty years to influence decisions and call all the shots.

Furthermore, the retired minister must fit in graciously with other members of the church staff, who are likely to be in the most formative years of their careers. Their positions should be honored, respected, and encouraged. Sensitivity toward their professional and growing needs must always be present, and never should the veteran minister seek to supplant or undermine their functions. Being a friend and a counselor, when called upon, are rewards enough.

3. Recycled pastors could easily experience the emotional crunch of spiritual regret and functional undernourishment. Their role is not to perform all the multifaceted functions of the ministry and enjoy all the ego-stroking gratifications. Having savored the "beloved pastor" feast in the past is no justification for greedily ransacking the banquet table now. Baptizing beautiful babies and officiating at beautiful weddings may no longer be realistic expectations. The sight of others enjoying these pastoral roles may cause recycled pastors to hemorrhage with sentimentality, but somewhere there must be a tourniquet of reality. The recycled pastor is

no longer cast in a starring role, but in a cameo part. It is not possible to eat one's retirement cake and have it too.

4. Recycled pastors must recognize that the aim of their ministry may necessarily be focused more narrowly. It is most likely that such persons will be called upon to spend a major portion of time in pastoral visitation. This calling may be on shut-ins, hospital patients, the elderly, and possibly prospective members. Here they must carefully assess their personal talents. If they do not enjoy, indeed, thrive on pastoral calling, this may be the wrong employment. Schaller estimates that since many pastors are naturally introverted, only about 30 or 40 percent actually enjoy pastoral calling. Carrying out a role one does not enjoy may prove onerous.

It has been asserted that the retired minister must be able to support the directing pastor in going about the assignments given. It is equally important, especially if the assignment is to call on prospective members, that the retiree be convinced that the congregation itself is viable and attractive. If one is expected to promote the congregation, one had better be satisfied that the congregation is a good "product." Otherwise, there is the risk of being seen as disingenuous.

One other function that might fall to the recycled minister is the teaching of an adult church school class. This was a privilege in both my post-retirement experiences. Since intellectual malnutrition may very well follow retirement, I find it stimulating to prepare for an adult class. This also becomes an outlet for the reservoir of knowledge and experience a pastor has built up over a lifetime. Continually, one hears the call of local churches for more adult instruction in the Bible. Many of our leading church officials suffer from biblical illiteracy, and adults of all ages express a deep need for this kind of learning. No one, other than the senior pastor, is better qualified to provide this teaching than a retired minister.

Many ministers dismember their personal libraries when they retire, either by selling or giving away the books, but retired ministers who find a new challenge in teaching should keep those libraries. They will find great need for books as the stimulus for further research and preparation is felt. Teaching a class may not be a substitute for the discipline of regular preaching, but the retired minister has, for the most part, hung up the pulpit gown.

But hold on! For some, there may come the opportunity for even further preaching on a regular basis. Just as I had decided I would never need to buy another pulpit gown, stitching up the old one with patches, a new stage of pastoral life has appeared—even in the twilight.

Seymour Halford, who already had recycled me as program minister, has taken seriously a bold suggestion in Lyle Schaller's recent book *44 Ways to Increase Church Attendance.* One of those 44 ways is the inauguration of an entirely different regular worship service, at a different hour, with a different preacher. Schaller believes that another preacher, with a different style and a differently styled liturgy, would attract significant numbers of new people. Obviously, such a scheme could be haunted with hazards, but my colleague is bold enough and sufficiently secure to give it a try. If it works, I may have to buy a new pulpit robe! I could become a recycled *preacher!* This proposal opens the floodgates for unlimited possibilities in retirement recycling.

5. Recycled status calls for careful consideration of the matter of tenure. How long should one continue in such a role? Perhaps there should be a formal contract. Just as with professional prize fighters, politicians, and athletes, the minister's sense of appropriate quitting time may become deadened. For a second time, the pastor may face the crucial decision—when should I retire?

The retired minister is not exempt from a principle here. One recycled pastor actually became a kind of embarrass-ment to the church. Though feeble and ineffective, he did not know enough to quit, and terminating him seemed to some cruel and insensitive. But because there was no contract and no offer on his part to leave, he went on for several years, exploiting the charity of the church, to be frank. That dear old minister was plainly worn out.

At the very beginning, it should be understood that a recycled pastor should come under scrutiny and review as careful as that for any other staff member. Diamonds may be forever, but recycled pastors need to know they are not.

One principle, I think, is clear: If the senior minister leaves a parish, the retired minister ought to automatically submit a resignation. The right of the incoming pastor to shape a new program and staff should be honored. Just as it may not be safe to retread an already retreaded tire, a minister must not assume immortal effectiveness.

Last, if one has felt, for forty years or so, the powerful challenge of preaching weekly sermons, a mature acceptance of one's new situation, which may possibly call for only an occasional sermon, is in order. The retiree must undergo a preacher's most demanding spiritual discipline: regularly hearing someone else preach. And without presumptuously offering homiletical hints. Unless requested. And if requested, the recycled pastor should carefully and clearly accent the positive. Some clergy might wait until asked, then see an opportunity to dump a whole load of criticism saved up for just such an occasion. Sitting in the pew can easily throw the retired minister into an ego fit, fantasizing that he or she could preach better, or at least differently. May these convulsive pew spasms be tranquilized in the gracious realization that one's pulpit robe belongs in the closet. Let the recycled one find gratification in supporting the preaching minister with goodwill and appreciation.

The retired minister does not need to be a salaried staff member to derive gratification in continuing ministry. One can be recycled usefully through volunteer service. One retiree who had a strong social-service emphasis in his preaching ministry volunteered to help cook and serve food at an inner-city mission. He loved doing it, and he was

109

practicing what he had preached for years. Many retired ministers volunteer to teach Sunday school, often employing their biblical and theological training and experience. In retirement, many are energized by this kind of continuing activity.

With the above cautions and observations, let it be asserted that there are blessings and benefits in being recycled. When I made the decision to retire, I did so deliberately, with full knowledge of the consequences. I like to think I knew what I was doing. I did not feel I was suffering clergy "burnout," and I did not want to be called a worn-out preacher. Given the realities of retirement, I am profoundly grateful for the privilege of continuing ministry on another level and a narrower track. And I am grateful that someone thought my gifts should be recycled. I don't mind being retreaded; I am learning to tread differently.

Recycling means reshaping one's ministry. And it may not be efficacious for everyone. But as the feverish years of one's life pass swiftly, and the shadows of the days lengthen, it is good to know that one need never cease being a minister of Jesus Christ. I would like to be able to sing as John Wesley sang on his deathbed:

> I'll praise my Maker while I've breath;
> And when my voice is lost in death,
> Praise shall employ my nobler powers.
> My days of praise shall ne'er be past,
> While life, and thought, and being last,
> Or immortality endures.